SURVIVING IN A BUOYANT ECONOMY

JOSEPH N. GLASGOW, PH. D

Surviving in a Buoyant Economy
Copyright © 2023 by Joseph N. Glasgow, Ph. D

ISBN: 978-1962497015 (sc)
ISBN: 978-1962497022 (e)

The Reading Glass Books
(888) 420-3050
production@readingglassbooks.com

TABLE OF CONTENTS

Surviving in a Buoyant Economy

This page was unintentionally left blank.

NOTES

It gives me immense pleasure and satisfaction to present my first book. Every effort has been made to avoid errors or omissions in this publication. It may, however, be noted that neither the publisher nor the author or seller will be responsible for any damage or loss of action to anyone, of any kind, in any manner, from that place. No part of this book may be reproduced or copied in any form or by any means (graphic, electronic or mechanical, including photocopying, recording, taping, or information retrieval systems) o r reproduced on any disc, tape, perforated media, or other information storage device, etc. without the written permission from the publisher. Breach of this condition is liable for legal action. THANK YOU!

This page was unintentionally left blank.

ACKNOWLEDGMENTS

I have come to realize that no one travels alone on an academic journey of life. Amazingly, where do I start to thank those, who accompanied me, traveled beside me, and helped me to walk every step of my way towards something that unceasingly urged me to write a book, to ink on a sheet of paper, or to document my thoughts which were acquired over the number of decades? Those I have met and worked with in my life. Here I wanted to share my insights and secrets to my continual, positive approach to life and all that life hurled at me. Ultimately, here is my book at last. So, perhaps this book and its content will be recognized as "thank you" to the very many thousands of you who have helped me make my life what it is today. Much of what I have learned over the years came as the result of my wife, who in her ways inspired me, and subconsciously contributed psychological support, for which I feel grateful. Thanks, Dorothy Jean, for your unwavering support.

Additionally, I also have to thank the late Hugh Harris (medical pharmacist/dispenser). Earlier in my adolescent life, he instilled in me the values of academic grounding to prosper. I also need to thank my wonderful parents (the late-Fitzhubert and Daphne Glasgow) who changed me completely, and they taught me humility and how to value the lives, thoughts, and expressions of others care for understand their needs. I also need to thank the faculty at the Cornell University (ILR) campus, State University of New York most notably mentors/faculties" Professors "Waltz Frytholm and Len Fela," two outstanding individuals."Central Michigan University, Northcentral University, and Western Carolina University, most notably Professor "Yang Fan, a remarkable person" Undoubtedly, it is through their teachings, encouragement, and support that I have gained and grown now. Through this book and my travels, I will continue to spread their message of support to others wishing to develop as human beings. It's strange to lament that I have been working non-stop for thirty-eight years and that this is my first book. The catalyst that made me complete this work was the ACLU American Civil Liberties Union. This fantastic organization comprises individuals with fantastic talent, all dedicated to sharing their knowledge with others to become successful in their future lives. They shared their knowledge, ideas, insight, and numerous tips, all of which culminated in completing this book. Thanks, guys. They helped me. They might also be of great help to you. Visit them at www.aclu.org

DESCRIPTION

It is an extraordinary book that talks boldly and vividly about our country's fluctuating or floating economy. The rise and fall of economic situations are based on the factors and influences caused by the micro and macro environment. The economic development of any country is based on developing the country's economic wealth and profit prioritization in the long term and the development of social welfare and public concerns. The business entities Co-operate with its environment, from which it receives the necessary resources and opportunities for its existence, growth, and survival. A business needs land and raw materials. The four factors of production are inputs used in various combinations for the production of goods and services to make an economic profit. The factors of production are land, labor, capital, and entrepreneurship. They are the inputs needed for supply. Mainly, the factors of production consist of any resource used in the creation of a good or service. Since these factors are limited by nature, and human wants are unlimited, we, as a country, face a decision over the efficient allocation of these scarce resources or factors of production. It also needs people to work, and it needs capital. All these resources come from the environment. In turn, the business must supply satisfactory returns to the environment. These returns are usually in the form of goods and services.

The sense that recent technological advances have yielded considerable benefits for everyday life, as well as disappointment over measured productivity and output growth in recent

years, has spurred widespread concern about whether our statistical systems are capturing these improvements. While concerns about measurement are not new to the statistical community, more people are now entering the discussion. More
economists are looking to do research that can help support
the statistical agencies. We explore the basic economics sur-
rounding the measurement of GDP, focusing, in particular, on
the question of whether GDP should be viewed as a measure of
aggregate economic well-being. Our exploration suggests that
while GDP, as currently defined, is not a comprehensive measure of welfare or even economic well-being, the GDP concept,
along with the pieces of GDP available through the national
accounts, is helpful in and of itself and should provide a great
deal of information that is closely related to welfare. Our finding that changes in real GDP does a reasonable job in capturing changes in economic wellbeing which has one important
exception; We argue that the exclusion of non-market activities
that bear on economic well-being merits more attention, particularly given the potential for changes in the importance of
such activities over time to change the degree to which changes
in GDP capture changes in well-being. This BOOK will provide an insight to the learners to understand how A Nations
Economy i s influenced and affected by this business environment and various other factors.

CHAPTER 1

INTRODUCTION

WHAT IS BUOYANT ECONOMY?

A buoyant economy is one in which there is a lot of trade and economic activity. It is a successful one in which people trust economic circumstances and expect an increase in income.

In a buoyant Economy, there is a lot of trade and economic activity as the economy is prospering. People have a sense of safety as their income is increasing.

GDP is now expected to increase 6.5% in 2021 before cooling off in later years, according to the Federal Open Market Committee, the central bank's monetary policy making group. That is sharply higher than the 4.2% forecast made in December.

The U.S. economic recovery paused at the end of 2020, but it will soon be ready for liftoff.... Households and firms alike are in good shape on average thanks to record stimulus in 2020 and another massive stimulus injection likely coming in 2021. We project U.S. real GDP growth of 5.3% in 2021 and 4% in 2022.

Consumer Confidence is an economic indicator that measures the degree of optimism consumers feel about the economy's overall state and personal financial situation. If the consumer has confidence in the immediate and near future Economy and his/her finance, then the consumer will spend more on expenditure than saving.

When consumer confidence is high, consumers make more purchases. When confidence is low, consumers tend to save more and spend less. A month-to-month trend in consumer confidence reflects consumers' outlook concerning their ability to find and retain good jobs according to their perception of the economy's current state and personal financial situation.

> The organization said Tuesday it expects the world economy to grow by 6% in 2021, up from its 5.5% forecast in January. Looking further ahead, global GDP for 2022 is seen increasing by 4.4%, higher than an earlier estimate of 4.2%.

Consumer confidence typically increases when the Economy expands and decreases when the Economy contracts. In the United States, there is evidence that the measure is a lagging indicator of stock market performance. The buoyant Economy can be measured with the help of the following attributes:

- Real per capita income
- Full employment
- Equal distribution of income
- Level of domestic and foreign debt

NATURE OF THE US ECONOMY:

The American Economy is best described as a "mixed economy," with government plays an essential role along with the involvement of private enterprise. A nation's primary ingredients are its natural resources, including fertile land and mineral resources. The US is rich in these natural resources and is also blessed with a moderate climate. Labor and enterprisers are considered essential resources, and the US has skilled labor that is very productive and efficient.

The US economy is the world's largest economy in the context of Nominal GDP. The US currency, i.e., the dollar, is used in international trade and internationally used as a reserve currency. The US financial markets are the most influential and most extensive in the world. The New York stock exchange is the world's largest stock exchange by market capitalization.

Economic growth, the process by which a nation's wealth increases over time. Although the term is often used in discussions of short-term economic performance, it generally refers to an increase in wealth over an extended period in the context of economic theory.

BUOYANT ECONOMY IN TERMS OF USA:

Let us discuss the attributes of a buoyant economy in terms of the USA economy:

Real Per Capita Income: Real per capita income refers to the measure of money earned per person in a particular area/economy. Per capita income can be obtained by dividing national income by population size. It refers to as a measure of prosperity.

The US has the world's seventh-highest Per Capita Income in the world. The US Census Bureau takes a survey of income per capita every ten years and revises it accordingly. The census includes earned income, salaries, wages, interest income, dividends, and government financial assistance. Then this data is used to estimate the per capita income of a particular area. The Higher value or per capita income means better living conditions and high quality of life.

Full Employment: Full employment is when all available labor resources are being used most efficiently. The labor resources include both skilled and unskilled amount of labor. Full employment means the employment level is rising, and unemployment rates are falling. Total nonfarm payroll employment rose by 266,000 in April, and the unemployment rate was little changed at **6.1 percent**, the U.S. Bureau of

Labor Statistics reported today. Notable job gains in leisure and hospitality, other services, and local government education were partially offset by employment. The last time the rate was this low was in December 1969, when it also was 3.5 percent. Over the month, the number of unemployed persons decreased by 275,000 to 5.8 million. The labor force participation rate came in at 63.2 percent, unchanged from the previous month. The unemployment rate in the United States averaged 5.74 percent from 1948 until 2019, reaching an all-time high of 10.80 percent in November of 1982 and a record low of 2.50 percent in May of 1953.

Despite this, there is always a natural rate of unemployment. The total employment number of the US is 155.6 million, and the unemployed number is 6.6 million.

Equal Distribution of Income: Income distribution refers to the equality and smoothness with which income is distributed among the people in an economy. Income distribution also tells about the wage pattern and average income of people. The higher the equality of income distribution, the higher will be economic stability. The term income includes wages, rent, interests, and profit.

Domestic And Foreign Debt: Foreign debt is the amount of debt a country owes to other countries (foreign countries), and domestic debt is the amount of debt owed to internal lenders. Foreign debt includes obligations to Asian Bank, International Monetary Fund, and World Bank, while domestic debt refers to Central and Commercial Banks or other financial institutions. The level of domestic debts can determine the level of buoyancy in an economy.

IS THE US ECONOMY A MIXED OR MARKET ECONOMY?

The US has a mixed market economy system. It has the characteristics of both capitalism and socialism. A Mixed Economy is designed to protect private property and allow economic freedom in the use of capital and resources. Still, at the same time, it allows the government to intervene to protect and promote social aims and public goods/commodities. The US government partially or alone controls many goods and services like health, education, justice, and infrastructure. The US government also provides a subsidy to various sectors of the economy, which is a perfect example of the US as a mixed economy. The US government encourages public-private enterprises by providing franchising and licensing some sectors to become more competitive and independent.

The main feature of a mixed Economy is the protection of consumer sovereignty. A consumer can buy and consume for which he can pay. The US economy is an example of this where consumer sovereignty is given preference, and consumers can get various goods and services.

A mixed Economy brings economic stability, just like in the case of the US economy. The private sector works under the guidance of price mechanism, i.e., market forces, and allocates resources to maximize its profit. The public a n d private sectors simultaneously own some productive resources. Sometimes, many producers produce different goods and services, making the problem of over production and production. The US government intervenes to solve the problem, which is a perfect example of a Mixed economy.

A mixed Economy ensures efficiency, which results in the mass production of goods and services. The allocation of resources by the private sector may lead to monopolies. Monopolies do not allow the allocation of resources efficiently. The government in a mixed Economy reduces such inefficiencies by reducing influences of monopolies, and the US government has strict policies to prevent monopolies like competition law, price capping, and price regulatory authorities. The US government also provides subsidies wherever it is warranted.

Mixed economies provide an equal opportunity to every person, and the US has equal rights for every person to consume and produce any commodity. Moreover, there are equal rights to everyone regarding health, education, and occupation.

The government is an active agent in a Mixed Economy. The prime aim of government is to provide social and economic justice to the people. The US government has various economic policies which are framed to promote the welfare of society.

There are also some demerits of a Mixed economy: Since both public and private sectors are actively engaged in a mixed economy, there may be a conflict between these two sectors. Sometimes, the public sector creates hurdles for the private sector, while sometimes, the private sector creates problems and challenges for the public sector.

Mixed Economy has no well-defined shape. Sometimes it tilts towards the free market and sometimes towards a planned economy.

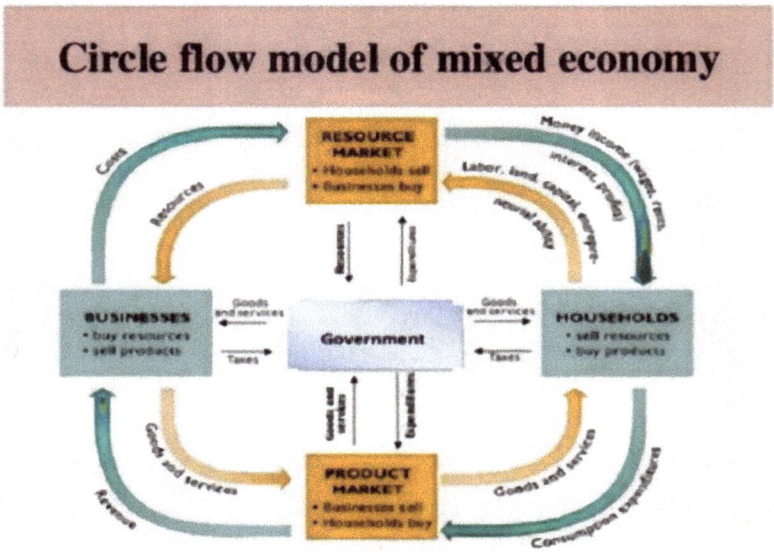

Circle flow model of mixed economy

TAXES AND TARIFFS AND THEIR IMPACT ON THE US ECONOMY:

Tax: Tax is a general compulsory contribution of wealth levied upon persons, natural or corporate, to defray the expenses incurred in conferring a common benefit upon the state's residents. Tax may be progressive, proportional, or regressive.

- A progressive tax is a tax or which tax rate increases with the increase in income. E.g., Income Tax. ➤ In proportional tax, the tax rate remains the same for all levels of income. E.g., License.
- A regressive tax is a tax in which the tax rate decreases with an increase in income. The burden of the tax falls heavily on the poor. The primary purpose of taxation is to collect revenue for the government and government expenditure. Taxes are the primary instrument of attaining specific social objectives. Taxes are mainly used as a part of fiscal policy.

ATTRIBUTES OF A GOOD TAX ARE (CANONS OF TAXATION):

- Equity: A tax should be equitable. Its burden should be more on the person who has more ability to pay. The progressive tax conforms to the principle of equity.
- Certainty: The income of the tax should be specific. The government needs reasonable resources to meet the fiscal requirements. The tax must generate the amount which is forecasted in the budget.
- Convenience: The mode of payment should be easy and convenient. A should be collected from the taxpayer at the time of his income. For example, agriculture tax should be collected at the time of harvest rather than the showing season.

- Economical: Most of the revenue collected from the tax should be deposited into the treasury. The cost of collection of the tax should come below.
- Diversity: several taxes should be imposed to generate more revenue. The indirect taxes increase the number of taxes and the number of people under the tax net, which increases the government's tax revenue.
- Simplicity: the methods of tax collection and the filing of tax returns should be simple and easy so that a typical taxpayer can understand them easily.
- Elasticity: The quality of good tax can be increased or decreased according to the economic conditions. Tariff: Tariff is a tax or duty which is paid on a particular class of imports. The purpose of the tariff is to increase imports, make them less desirable and least competitive in the market, and ultimately encourage the consumption of domestic goods. Tariff is also a way to increase government revenue, and this revenue is then used to promote a particular industry.

TYPES OF TARIFFS:

- A specific tariff is levied as a fixed fee upon particular items.
- An ad-valorem whose levy is based on the value of the items. Like 20% of the value of the item.

Free trade promotes the level of economic output and barriers like tariff economic output and income. Tariffs usually raise the price of goods and reduce available quantities of goods and services.

IMPACT OF TAXES AND TARIFF ON THE US ECONOMY:

The US government imposes various taxes to create revenue for public expenditures and finance its operations like income tax, sales tax, excise tax, property tax, capital gain tax, etc. In a buoyant economy taxes and tariff plays an important role. The increase in real per capita income means that the income of people is rising, and they have to pay more tax than previously. The government may expect an increase in revenue and spend it on public expenditure and welfare.

Taxes are the primary tool for the circular flow of income. In the US economy, every individual has a sense of responsibility to pay tax because the government used these taxes to provide necessities like health and education. Tariff discourages imports, and a high tariff rate helps an economy avoid foreign debt and prefers domestic production.

GDP/GNP:

GDP: Gross Domestic Product is the value of goods and services within an economy in a given period, usually a year. It is an income derived from domestic economic activities. It is a significant contribution to the national income and is measured by the gross value of the asset, i.e., without deducting depreciation on fixed assets. Amongst other models of various national income measures, GDP is the most reliable and important one. This is because of the difficulty of allowing for depreciation on fixed capital. Further, it takes preference over other national products of the delay and difficulty measuring the net flow of property income from abroad.

GDP = Consumption + Government Expenditure + Investments + (Exports – Imports)

GDP: is an important indicator to gauge the health of a country's economy. GDP is also used to measure the size of the Economy by measuring the total dollar value of all goods and services. GDP is usually expressed as a comparison to the previous quarter/year. According to the Bureau of Economic Analysis, United States of America, GDP increased at the annual rate of 6.2% in the fourth quarter of 2021. The overall growth of 2021 compared to the previous year was 6.2%.

The US economy is ranked as the world's biggest economy and ranked as # 1 since 1871. In 2021, the size of the US economy was estimated at $60.39 trillion in nominal terms, and it was expected to reach $20.41 trillion in 2018. The US economy is a service-oriented economy that contributes 80% of its total GDP, while the manufacturing sector only contributes 15% of its output.

GNP: Gross National Product means GDP plus income accruing to domestic residents from investment abroad minus income accruing to foreign residents from investment in the domestic economy.

> **GNP = GDP + Net Property Income from Abroad**

> **GNP is the total monetary value of the output produced by a country.** Any output produced by foreign residents within the national boundary is not included in the GNP calculation, while output produced by national residents in the foreign boundary should be included.

The US government used GNP to measure its economic activity until 1991; the US started using GDP to give more precise results.

FACTOR WHICH INFLUENCES US GDP/ GNP:

In 2017, the US GDP and GNP were estimated at $60.39 trillion and $19.69 trillion. The significant difference between GNP and GDP may indicate that country is becoming more engaged in international trade, production, or financial operation.

Economic analysis provides an insight into the essentials of an economy. Economic growth refers to the long-term expansion of the productive potential of the economy, which ultimately satisfies the wants of individuals. If there is sustainable economic growth, it will have a strong positive effect o n national income and unemployment, which results in higher living standards. Economic growth plays an essential role in stimulating government finances by enhancing tax revenues. It enables the government to earn extra income for the further development of the country. Following are some determinants that influence GDP/GDP:

- Human Resources: The availability of human resources can directly affect the growth of an economy. It can be measured as both qualitative and quantitative. Quality of human resources refers to skills, creative abilities, training, and education. The quantity can be referred to as how much labor is willing to work, i.e., level of employment. US has a high quality of labor which has a significant contribution to its GDP.
- Natural Resources: Natural resources include resources on land and beneath the land. On land, resources are the forest, land resources, and water resources. The resources beneath the land are natural gas, crude oil, minerals, metals, and non-metals. The utilization of natural resources depends on the availability of human resources, funds, and the use of technology. US country is rich with human and natural resources, which ensure its economic growth.
- Capital Formation: Capital formation includes infrastructure, land, buildings, power sources, and communications mode. Capital formation increases the availability of capital per worker and increases real income per capita. Consequently, the productivity of labor increases which increases the output and growth of the Economy.
- Technological development: Technology refers to the use of the scientific application and modern

production techniques. Technology development helps in increasing productivity with the limited amount of resources. Countries like the USA that have worked in technological development have rapid growth and a higher GDP than countries with less focus on technological development.

- Social and Political Factors: Social and political factors play a crucial role in economic growth. Social factors are customs, beliefs, traditions, core values, and working habits that contribute to the economy considerably. Political factors like government participation in formulating policies and implementing them have a significant effect on economic growth.

CPI: Inflation means the rise in the general price level. The rate of inflation means the rate of change in the general price level. The price index measures the average change in the price of goods and services over time. A simple price index is calculated as:

Pon = Pn / Po x 100
Pn = Price in Current Year
Po = Price in Base Year

Consumer Price Index (CPI) measures the average change in price over time in the standard basket of consumer goods and services. The standard basket of goods and services includes food and beverages, clothing, housing, fuel and transport, medical care, education, and other goods and servicespurchased for daily consumption.

The consumer price index is calculated by weighing the price according to the importance of a commodity.

CPIn = CPI(n-1) x Weighted Change in Prices in Period n

CPI is the statistical estimate calculated using the price of consumer goods and services from the consumer baskets. The goods are divided into categories, and a sample of goods is selected from each category, representing the whole category. Sub-indices are calculated for category and sub-category. The results calculated show the overall index with weights and reflecting their shares in the total of the consumer expenditures covered by the index. The annual change in percentage of CPI is used as the measure of inflation.

CPI AND THE US ECONOMY:

Bureau of Labor Statistics (BLS), United States, is responsible for calculating the CPI's for different goods and services. BLS publishes the CPI results monthly. The BLS started this calculation in 1919 and provided statistics regularly.

The statistics provided by BLS are used as an economic indicator. CPI is a measure of inflation; the CPI measures government fiscal and monetary policy effectiveness. The CPI statistics are used by entrepreneurs, labor markets, and other private citizens in making economic decisions.

G20 COUNTRIES:

G20 or a group of twenty consists of 20 countries (Argentina, Australia, Brazil, Canada, China, France, Germany, India, Indonesia, Italy, Japan, Mexico, Russia, Saudi Arabia, South Africa, South Korea, Turkey, the United Kingdom, Shinzo Abe, and the United States) and European Union.G20 countries are two-third of the world population and account for significant exports. The purpose of g20 is to provide facilitation to the governments and central banks of all the countries and the European Union to discuss policy about promoting international financial stability and bringing together all the economic Cooperation.

Influence on the US Economy: The influence of the G20 on the US economy can be measured with the help of the following attributes.

- Economy stability and sustainable growth
- Allies with other economic cooperation
- Financial stability
- Women's empowerment
- Environment

Economic Development in the US: The few years have witnessed dramatic gains in the standard of living in the United States, driven by the technological innovation introduced by the industrial revolution and carried forward by the evolution of technology since then. Examining US economy growth provides us that GDP grew at an annual rate of 3.2%. The strong growth in volume and variety of imports from the rest of the G20 nations has allowed the United States to boost its economy in terms of industry and technology. Rising consumer incomes, international trade agreements, and improved technology have led to substantial growth in the demand and supply of goods and services following the volume and variety of US products and services. US imports most of its products from China, Canada, India, and Japan, which are G20 countries. The US imported $147 billion worth of Chinese goods which is 41.83% (by value) of US purchases from china, and $75.4 billion vehicles purchases from Canada, which is 16.4% of total import. In 2016, The US also imported $68.8 billion of machinery, including computers from Canada and $356 billion (barrels) of oil from different countries within the G20. G20 forum provides US country to make agreements with other member countries leading to economic cooperation.

ALLIES WITH OTHER ECONOMIC COOPERATION:

G20 forum also provides allies with other countries and supports young entrepreneurs. At the beginning of 2016, G20 played an essential role in resolving China and America's economic and trade clash. Over 40 years, the US and China have developed an interdependent economic and extensive cooperative political relationship. The optimistic tone of the G20 forum generates hope that China and America may yet avoid the Thucydides Trap (which postulates the inevitability of a clash between an established and rising power). The G20's primary focus has been the governance of global alliances. It helps the US lead the business and encourage relationships with other economic cooperation like china, Korea, and Canada. Rotation of presidency each year in December allows a different G20 member country to assume the group's presidency. The president is chosen through a system of rotation. All countries can take over the G20 presidency within a group when it is their group's turn.

FINANCIAL STABILITY:

Financial stability is the ability to withstand a temporary problem. It is essential because it determines what tool you can use to address financial stability issues, for this domestic law must be implemented across the borders. It would be best if you were in a stable position to grow. Based on this approach, the US considers the lifecycle in its entirety. An economy with reasonably constant output and low profit, and stable inflation would be considered a financially stable income in its economic country.

WOMEN EMPOWERMENT:

G20 international forum also provides an opportunity for women to self- organization and self-managed savings group, develop their empowerment, and increase their access to financial resources, which is helpful to sustained poverty alleviation. G20 provide opportunity in the US and many other countries to be an entrepreneur. It also enhances the inbuilt skills to ensure sustainability. According to the international forum, women are key to drive growth and sustainability. However, the possibility for women's rights has seen little growth.

ENVIRONMENT:

G20 stepped up to address the climate change challenges. It put massive strides in recycling or redirecting solid waste from landfills. On this approach, the US uses recyclable packing for its majority of products and ties many organizations' compensation to their sustainability practices. Besidesthe environmental impact, the US environmental policies also focus on the company's employee treatment, ethical leadership, and transparent customer service.

INFLUENCE OF PUBLIC/PRIVATE SECTOR ON THE US ECONOMY:

It is impossible to assess the overall impact of public-private partnerships on general economic growth. A public-private partnership is likely to increase n e t investment in a particular sector and generate more projects in a particular sector. It is uncertain that these funds are more productive in other parts of the Economy. Its impact depends on the opportunity costs involved. Public-private partnerships are usually found in transport infrastructures, such as roads, airports, railroads, bridges, waterways and tunnels, municipal corporations, environmental infrastructures such as water and wastewater facilities.

Public services include school buildings, prisons, student residences, and entertainment or sports facilities. Economic growth can be achieved by investment and increases in productive potential, allowing individual workers to gain more excellent value for their work and achieve a higher living standard.

A series of seismic changes fundamentally change how we should consider promoting the relationship between public and private flows to promote development. This change is reflected in former President Obama's administration policies, but US aid programs have not emerged enough to exploit the new development landscape. The majority of development actors, including those in the private sector, continue to be transported as if 87% of private development flows were needed to develop the way of working with t h e public. A new attitude should focus on the areas in which Official Development Assistance (ODA) adds unique value. This is probably where ODA completes another private stream. Public service support will need to engage effectively with the private sector in joint development initiatives in agreed-upon areas and be a constructive force for a more robust political environment that attracts more private capital. The first may include sharing knowledge and best practices with private sector partners. The second may include strengthening investments in infrastructure, market creation, and institutions.

ECONOMIC FACTS AND EFFECTS THAT IMPACT THE US ECONOMY:

The United States is a union of fifty American states. It has had the world's largest Economy in the world since,1987. (https://www.un.org/en/development/desa/policy/wess/wess_archive/searchable_ It is a mixed economy. This means that it acts as a free market economy for consumer goods and business services. Well, even in these areas, the government imposes regulations to protect the interests of all. It is a dominant economy in the defense sector, some pension benefits, some medical care, and many other areas. The United States Constitution creates a mixed American economy. Where Some Quick Facts of the US economy are:

- Gross domestic product: $ 21.34 trillion (annual nominal rate for the second quarter of 2019)
- GDP growth rate: 2.1% (annual rate for the second quarter of 2019)

- GDP per capita: $ 57,800 (second quarter 2019) Federal Reserve of St. Louis
- Gross national income: $ 19.872 trillion PPP (2017) The World Bank
- Unemployment rate: 3.7% for July 2019
- Minimum wage: $ 7.25 per hour
- Currency: US dollar Converting
- Euro to Dollar: 1.11 USD since August 2019
- Inflation: heart rate of 2.1% year after year for June 2019

CLIMATE EFFECTS ON THE US ECONOMY:

Climate change should be called climate destabilization. This creates more severe and frequent snow storms, heat waves and other forms of severe weather. This includes tornadoes, forest fires, hurricanes, snow storms floods and landslides, heat waves and droughts. It also includes heavy storms, whether dust, hail, rain, snow or ice and US is already facing these circumstances and earn a huge amount of loss due to migration and other related issues.

A 2017 survey showed that 55% of Americans believe that climate change has accelerated hurricanes. As a result, 48% said they were afraid of climate change. (https://www.thebalance.com/economic-impact-of-climatechange- 3305682)

There is indeed no new climate change in the history of the Earth. On the other hand, previous changes have occurred over millions of years, not yesterday.

IMPACT OF CHINESE ECONOMY ON THE US ECONOMY:

China is the third-largest export partner (the first and the second with Canada and Mexico, respectively) in the United States. The United States with export goods and services total $ 129.9 billion in 2017, according to the US Trade Representative in the Obama trade administration. This represents 8.4% of total US exports during this period.

China is also the leading importing partner of the United States, whose imports have been valued at the US $ 505.5 billion since 2017, or about 21.6% of total US imports. As a result, the United States trade balance with China was negative, and China's capital flows partly finance this deficit.

China was also the largest creditor in the United States and held most US Treasury securities. They have reached $ 1.18 billion since 2018. According to US Treasury data in April 2018, this represented 21% of US foreign debt. The statistics above show the Chinese economy's importance and explain why any evolution of China, whether negative or positive, can affect the most significant economy globally, said the United States US treasury Department.

A MANAGEMENT STRUCTURE THAT DEPICTS A TYPICAL OFF-SHORE MNC (MULTINATIONAL CORPORATION):

A multinational corporation has other facilities and assets in at least one country other than its country of origin. These companies have offices and factories in different countries and have a centralized headquarters to coordinate global management. Large multinational companies have higher budgets than many small countries in which they operate.

Multinational corporations are sometimes called transnational, international, or non-state corporations.

As a general rule, multinational corporations generate at least a quarter of their income outside their home country. Many multinational companies have been established in developed countries like USA. Multinational companies a r e creating well-paid jobs and state-of-the-art products in countries that would not have access to such opportunities or assets. Conversely, Trade critics and Economic pundits echoed say that multinational companies have unduly political influence on governments, that developing countries are used, and create job losses in their countries. According to the Fortune Global 500 List, the 10 largest multinational corporations in the world as of 2017 are:

- Walmart ($500.34 billion)
- State Grid ($348.90 billion)
- Sinopec Group ($326.95 billion)
- China National Petroleum ($326.01 billion)
- Royal Dutch Shell ($311.87 billion)
- Toyota Motor ($265.17 billion)
- Volkswagen ($260.03 billion)
- BP ($244.58 billion)
- ExxonMobil ($244.36 billion) and
- Berkshire Hathaway ($242.14 billion).

MNC AND THE US ECONOMY:

US multinational companies are, first and foremost, American companies. T h e y perform large shares of America's productivity-enhancing capital investment, research and development, and trade, leading to jobs and high compensation. The central role of US multinational companies in underpinning US economic growth and job creation is even more critical today as the United States seeks to address the challenges presented by the ongoing deep recession. Strong US multinational companies that can compete effectively in foreign markets will be better positioned to help restore American economic growth.

The ability of US multinationals to stem domestic job losses and return to hiring more American workers depends on the health, vitality, and competitiveness of their worldwide operations. (https://www.businessroundtable.org/archive/resources/how-u.s.- multinational-companies-strengthen-the -u.s.-economy-data-update)

At the same time, US multinationals are becoming more inte-grated and connected. Parent companies and foreign affiliates are so dynamic, numerous, and essential that parent companies and affiliates are often confused with diversity. The global success of US multinationals depends more and more on its global presence and global competitiveness, with dynamic diversity in both successful strategies about companies at a point in time and within companies over time.

Global competitiveness requires US Multinationals to establish off-shore operations, grow abroad, and integrate these activities abroad with their parent companies. International countries generally support multinational companies abroad to support their activities in America. Instead of replacing, the external affiliation activity completes the main activities of a parent company in the United States are paid compensation and investing in workers. The main idea of global expansion is the improved US operations in multinational enterprises and increasing its productivity and the average standard of living of all Americans.

INTELLECTUAL PROPERTY AND THE US ECONOMY:

Intellectual Property (IP) relates to the formation of the mind, such as inventions, literary and artistic works, drawings, and the symbols, names, and images used in the trade.

Intellectual property is legally protected, for example, through patents, copyrights, and trademarks, which allow individuals to be recognized or financially benefit from what they have created or created. By maintaining t h e right balance between the interests of innovators and the general interest, the IP system aims to create an environment conducive to creativity and innovation.

The protection of intellectual property (IP) affects commerce across the Economy by providing incentives to create and care protect innovators from unauthorized copying, facilitating vertical specialization in technology markets; creating a platform for financial investments in innovation; supporting liquidity and start-up growth through mergers, acquisitions, and IPOs. Business models based on licensing technology enable a more efficient technology transfer and trading technology and ideas.

On September 26, 2016, the US Department of Commerce published a full report entitled "US Intellectual Property and

Economy: 2016 Update," which indicated that the industry supported intensive intellectual property with at least $ 45 million jobs in the United States and contributed more than $ 6 billion, or 38.2% of the gross domestic product (GDP) of the United States. The report, a joint product of the United States Patent and Trademark Office (USPTO) and the Economic and Statistical Administration (ESA), updates t h e report on the intellectual Economy and the state of Economy in newspapers March 2012.

The report contains several important conclusions, including:

- The intense IP industries continue to be an integral part of the US economy.
- This report identifies 81 industries (out of a total of 313) in intense intellectual property. These IP-intensive industries generated 27.9 million jobs in 2014, 0.8 million more than in 2010.
- The intensive brand industries represent the most significant number of people and employ most jobs, with 23.7 million jobs in 2014 (22.6 million in 2010). The copyright industries generated 5.6 million jobs (compared to 5.1 million in 2010), followed by intensive patent industries with 3.9 million jobs (3.8 million in 2010).
- While employment in IP-intensive industries increased between 2010 and 2014, non-intensive IP jobs grew at a slightly faster pace. As a result, total employment in IP-intensive industries decreased slightly from 18.8% in 2010 to 18.2%.
- In contrast, value-added by IP-intensive industries increased significantly i n total share and GDP between 2010 and 2014. Intellectual property density industries generated $ 6.6 billion in value-added in 2014, more than $ 1.5 billion (30%) of $ 5.06 billion in 2010. As a result, the share of total US GDP attributable to the intensive intellectual property sector increased from 34 8% in 2010 to 38.2% in 2014.

- Specific revenues related to intellectual property rights licenses amounted to $ 115.2 billion in 2012, while 28 industries earned these licenses.

CHAPTER 2

NATURE OF THE US ECONOMY

For thousands and thousands of years, life was, in the evocative language of Thomas Hobbes, "nasty, brutish, and short." Only in the last two centuries has this changed, but the change has been dramatic in this relatively brief time. Looking back over more than a century of political and economic developments, Anton Brender and Florence Pisani document the continuing economic leadership of the US and the increasing gulf between labor and capital that has left the US economy polarized as its politics. They assert that this is accepted due to a cultural 'aversion to public intervention'. But only by revisiting this stance can the whole of the US hope to prosper in a world of increasing international competition and continuous technological progress. However, the use of fiscal and, more recently, monetary policy, although successful in rapidly re-establishing full employment, has done little to offset the increasing inequality that undermines both the country's growth potential and social harmony. It presents an analytical framework motivated by empirical evidence and embeds the conventional approaches to economic growth.

The United States is rich in mineral ore resources and fertile farm soil, and it is blessed with a moderate climate. It also has extensive coastlines on both the Atlantic and Pacific Oceans and the Gulf of Mexico. Rivers flow from far within the continent, and the Great Lakes five large, inland lakes along the US border with Canada provide additional shipping access. These extensive waterways have helped shape the country's economic growth over the years and helped bind America's 50 individual states together in a single economic unit.

Since the 1970s, the American Economy is experiencing increasing difficulty in generating social progress. How can this paradox be explained? Answering this question is the thread running throughout this book, which offers an overview of the history and structure of the American Economy, guided by a concern to shed light on the problems it faces today. The distress associated with the rise in mass unemployment obliged the federal government to establish institutions that are still today at the heart of American social solidarity arrangements.

Consumer spending by households is the main component of American domestic demand. Today it accounts for more than two-thirds of GDP, compared with only 60% at the beginning of the 1950s. In seven decades, its composition has undergone substantial changes. The share of services rose by almost 30 percentage points, and non-durables (food and clothing) fell by 27 points, while durable goods fell by only 2 points. The shift in relative prices referred to earlier plays a significant role in this respect. Despite the spectacular evolution in the share of services in household spending, the 'volume' of the services consumed rose in line with consumption as a whole.

When durable goods were declining slightly as a share of households' spending, in volume terms, their consumption of these goods has risen distinctly faster than that of services, driven mainly by spectacular growth i n purchases of electronic and computer-related goods. The "recreational goods" of which they form part now account for a larger share of durable good s purchases than furnishing and household equipment and are approaching the level of automobiles. The impressive slump in the proportion of spending devoted to purchases of non-durable goods is explained, in part at least, by a growth in volume that is smaller than that of total consumption. This unfavorable tendency in terms of volume was compounded by the fact that the evolution in prices was also less rapid than for consumption as a whole.

Between 1947 and 2016, the share of financial services in household consumer spending has, for its part, risen substantially, from less than 3% to almost 8%.

First, for 75 years, educational attainment rose steadily, at a rate of slightly less than one year per decade. For example, the cohort born in 1880 got just over seven years of education, while the cohort born in 1950 received 13 years of education on average. Between 1940 and 1980, for example, educational attainment rose from 9 years to 12 years or about 3/4 of a year per decade. With a return to education of 7%, this corresponds to a contribution of about 0.5 percentage points per year to growth in output per worker.

The other fact that stands out prominently, however, is the leveling-off of educational attainment. For cohorts born after 1950, educational attainment rose more slowly than before, and for the latest cohorts, educational attainment has essentially flattened out.

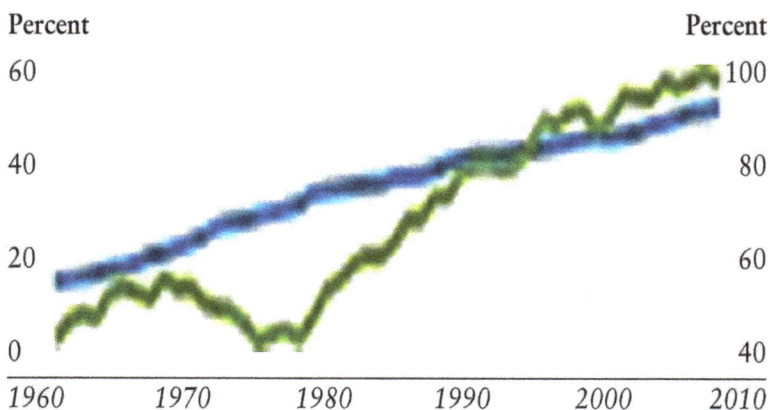

Fig. 1 The supply of college graduates and the college wage premium, 1963–2012. Note: The supply of US college graduates, measured by their share of total hours worked, has risen from below 20% to more than 50%

by 2012. The US college wage premium is calculated as the average excess amount earned by college graduates relative to no graduates, controlling for experience and gender composition within each educational group. Source: Author, D.H. 2014. Skills, education, and the rise of earnings inequality among the "other 99 percent."

Various growth models have been developed to explain the transition from stagnant living standards for thousands of years to the modern era of economic growth. Because of its size and international linkages, developments in the US economy are bound to have substantial implications for the global economy. For several decades now, the American Economy has been leading the way both for the most advanced economies and for others that have been rapidly making up their backlogs. To that end, the development of its economy has been based on a social order that still retains a somewhat original character, is profoundly rooted in the values of the "founding fathers" who at the end of the eighteenth century achieved independence of the United States from British domination and "conservatism."

Their preference for non-intervention was based on an ideology that differed from that prevalent in European countries.

At first glance, it appears that patents, like many other variables, have grown exponentially. Indeed, at least since 1980, one sees a very dramatic rise in the number of patents granted in the United States, both in total and US inventors. The foreign patenting in the United States is also enjoyable. One testament to the global nature of ideas is that 56% of patents granted by the US patent office in 2013 were foreigners.

The United States is a large producer of consumer commodities. It has re- emerged as the largest oil and natural gas producer in recent years, accounting for 13 percent of global oil production (similar to its share in the early 1990s). US production is almost evenly split between natural gas and petroleum, in contrast to the predominantly petroleum-based production of other major hydrocarbon producers such as Russia and Saudi Arabia (EIA 2016). US shale oil production, which tripled during 2009-14, requires little capital investment and can be brought on stream rapidly; hence, it has become a highly flexible source of global oil supply, responding quickly to price changes (Baffes et al. 2016).

The United States is also the world's largest biofuel producer, accounting for 42 percent of global production. Rapid growth in maize-based production was encouraged by the Renewable Fuel Standard (RFS), mandated by the Energy Policy Act of 2005 and the Energy Independence and Security Act of 2007, which requires transportation fuel sold in the United States to contain a minimum volume of renewable fuels.

Historically, the United States has been a significant consumer of agricultural, energy, and metal commodities. With the rise of large EMDEs, such as China and India, this role has diminished over time (World Bank 2015a). However, the United States is still the largest consumer of natural gas and oil, accounting for more than one-fifth of global consumption. It is the second-largest consumer of a wide range of commodities, including aluminum, copper, lead, and coffee.

International business cycle synchronization tends to be particularly strong when the US economy is in recession. Over the phases of the US business cycle, GDP growth in the rest of the world substantially correlates with the US cycle. For example, growth was on average higher in other advanced economies and EMDEs during periods of US expansions than it was when the US economy was in recession. More importantly, although the four recessions the global Economy experienced since 1960 (1975, 1982, 1991, and 2009) were driven by a host of problems in many corners of the world, they all overlapped with severe recessions in the United States.

The global recession of 1975 coincided with the beginning of a prolonged period of stagflation, with low output growth and high inflation in the United States. During the 1982 recession, the United States and several other advanced economies experienced a sharp decline in activity along with a steep increase in unemployment in the wake of anti-inflationary monetary policies. The economy again went into recession in July 1990 following a period of depressed activity in the housing market and a credit crunch. The deep global recession of 2009 was driven by the global financial crisis, which had its origins in the US mortgage market but turned into a truly global crisis after the collapse of Lehman Brothers in September 2008. These four US recessions coincided with global recessions; there were. However, four other US recessions post-1960 did not.

Our exploration suggests that while GDP, as currently defined: is not a comprehensive measure of welfare or even economic well-being, the GDP concept, along with the pieces of GDP available through the national accounts, is helpful in and of itself and should provide a great deal of information that is closely related to welfare. Our finding that changes in real GDP do a reasonable job in capturing economic well-being changes has one important exception. We argue that the exclusion of non-market activities that bear on economic well-being merits more attention, particularly given the potential for changes in the importance of such activities over time to change the degree to which changes in GDP capture changes in well-being. Moreover, there are several important areas where measurement falls short of the conceptual ideal. First, the national accounts may measure the nominal GDP arising from the Digital Economy and the operation of multinationals corporations. Second, the deflators used to separate GDP into nominal GDP and real GDP may produce a biased measure of inflation. Our analysis suggests that, for goods and services that do not change in quality over time, current deflator methods work reasonably well. But, current methods may not capture consumer surplus for new goods and services or goods in services that are changing in quality. We believe that efforts to improve price measurement to measure consumer welfare should be pursued. Such a measure would be very useful for understanding the current state of the Economy and policymaking.

Developments in the US economy have significant impacts on the global economy. Shocks to the US economy transmit to the rest of the world through the range of channels discussed above. Given its sizable role in global commodity markets, acceleration in US activity tends to lift global commodity demand and raise prices. This supports activity and eases balance of payments pressures in commodity exporters. Financial market developments in the United States may have even broader global implications. Therefore, US policies could affect the domestic activity and generate wide-ranging cross-border spillovers through real and financial channels.

More people are now entering the discussion and more economists are looking to do research that can help support the statistical agencies. The starting point for these efforts should be a basic understanding of how the statistics are defined and how they are limited, both in terms of the concept and in terms of how they are calculated given the concept. While much of this information can be found in writings by experts and scholars on economic statistics, this literature is extensive in volume and often hard to understand by non-experts, even other economists.

CHAPTER 3

BUOYANT ECONOMY IN
TERMS OF USA

The last decade has been a perfect one for developing countries and their mostly poor citizens so good that it has become common to look upon them as potential saviors of the World's Economic. Their economies have expanded at unprecedented rates, resulting in a large reduction in extreme poverty and a significant middle-class expansion. Recently, the differential between the growth rates of developing and advanced countries expanded to more than five percentage points, assisted in part by the decline in the economic performance of the rich countries. A strong dollar creates instability in the commodity market, as most commodities are traded in US dollars. This puts enormous pressure on countries where growth largely depends on the export of commodities. The US economy is thriving. Its GDP growth rate is above 3%. The first three quarters of 2018 saw 2.2%, 4.2%, and 3.5%, respectively. Unemployment is below 4%, and October's 3.7% is the lowest since 1969.

It is the determinants of this transformation of the US economy into a 'tertiary' economy that will now be described before examining the consequences for employment and the formation of household income.

The first is the development of fundamental capabilities in the form of human capital and institutions. Long-term growth ultimately depends on the accumulation of these capabilities, The policies needed to accumulate fundamental capabilities and those required to foster structural change naturally overlap, but they are distinct. The first types of policies entail a much broader range of investments in skills, education, administrative capacity, and governance; the second can take the form of narrower, targeted remedies.

A) REAL PER CAPITA INCOME:

The Bureau of Economic Analysis (BEA) gives a clear definition for GDP: Gross domestic product (GDP) is the value of the goods and services produced by the nation's economy, less the value of the goods and services used up in production. GDP is also equal to the sum of personal consumption expenditures, gross private domestic investment, net exports of goods and services, government consumption expenditures, and gross investment.

With an estimated nominal GDP of more than $18 trillion in 2016, the United States is the world's single largest economy and has the world's third- largest population. It accounts for more than 25 percent of global GDP (at 2015 market exchange rates), 11 percent of global trade, 12 percent foreign bank claims, and 35 percent of global stock market capitalization. The US share of global output and trade has remained broadly stable since the 1980s, whereas the share of other major advanced economies has declined gradually. The United States is the single largest international creditor and debtor: it holds the largest stock of foreign assets and liabilities and, by a wide margin, the largest net foreign asset position.

The United States is the world's single largest Economy (at market exchange rates), accounting for almost 22 percent of global output and over a third of stock market capitalization. It is prominent in virtually every global market, accounting for about one-tenth of global trade flows, one-fifth of global FDI stock, close to one-fifth of remittances, and one-fifth of global energy demand. For nearly

150 years, GDP per person in the US economy has grown at a remarkably steady average rate of around 2% per year. Starting at around $3,000 in 1870, per capita GDP rose to more than $50,000 by 2014, a nearly 17-fold increase.

The Gross Domestic Product per capita in the United States was last recorded at 54541.70 US dollars in 2021.

Trade accounted for 28 percent of US GDP in 2015, considerably less than the average for other advanced economies (70 percent) but significantly more prominent than in the 1980s (18 percent). The United States is the world's single largest importer and exporter of goods and services and the largest exporter and importer of business services. It accounts for 14 percent of global goods imports and 9 percent of global services imports.

The current expansion is now one of the longest on record. Economic growth since the financial crisis has also been amongst the strongest. However, similar to other countries, productivity growth has been sluggish and below the growth rates recorded during previous expansions. As a result, the expansion has also been one of the weakest over the past half-century. In part, weak investment growth also by State and local governments has contributed to this outcome. The expansion has been one of the longest on record. Material wellbeing is high and Americans are doing well on average in comparison with residents of other countries.

The United States performs favorably compared to the rest of the country, particularly for measures of disposable income and household wealth, long- term unemployment and housing conditions. And the recovery from the crisis has led to marked gains in consumer confidence.

On the other hand, gains in life expectancy since the 1960s have been moderate compared to countries, and attaining a good work-life balance appears a particular issue for American workers. Consumer confidence is high. The near-term outlook is strong. Private consumption remains solid, bolstered by the strong labor market, wealth gains, and high consumer confidence levels. In the business sector, confidence is also robust, and business fixed investment is picking up. The tax will further boost business investment.

The growth effects of the fiscal stimulus are expected to boost revenues and the taxation on the deemed repatriation of foreign profits will give a temporary boost to revenues. In addition, the tax reform may attract inward investment and reduce corporate inversions and outward investment. However, action will be needed to ensure fiscal sustainability if revenue and spending growth fail to attain the rates underpinning the Administration's budget forecasts. The policy recommendations made in this Survey would also entail additional fiscal costs.

B) FULL EMPLOYMENT:

The maintenance, against all odds, of relatively full employment was made possible by continuous growth in private borrowing. However, this accumulation of debt was not accompanied by the increased surveillance of the financial system, as it should have been. Here again, the aversion to public intervention inspired the belief that 'market discipline' would be sufficient to prevent any collapse on the financial markets.

Robust job growth has helped bring people back into employment and has reduced the unemployment rate. Employment growth above the rates needed to account for new entrants into the labor force has reduced unemployment to historically low levels, which has resulted in tight labor markets for fast- growing locations and occupations. Together with more substantial wage gains, these trends have helped partially reverse the decline in real median household income since the recession. However, employment as a share of the population has still not fully recovered from the crisis. Unemployment is now very low.

- For almost four decades the average annual growth in real wages in fact barely exceeded 1%, as against productivity growth of close to 2%. This tendency is explained by the interplay of two forces of different kinds.
- The first relates to the warping of the distribution of private sector firms' value added in favor of profits, whose

share of the total rose by more than three percentage points between the early 1980s and the mid-2010s.

- The second relates to an evolution in relative prices that is also to the detriment of the purchasing power of wages, with the prices of goods and services consumed by American households tending to rise more rapidly than those of corporate value-added.

The relative size of the American middle class defined as the proportion of households earning between two-thirds and twice the median disposable income is now smaller than anywhere else (Kochhar, 2017), partly as a result of the increase in the proportion of the most disadvantaged (those earning less than two-thirds of the median income)!

Here again, the populations most affected are the least qualified: the mortality rate for whites in the 50-54 group with no more than a high school diploma has substantially increased. Note, however, that while the mortality rate for fifty-year-old has continued to fall in the case of the Hispanic population and even more for the black population, for the latter it remained substantially higher than for the rest of the population.

However, the same cannot be said of the median wage: in fact, for almost forty years, the purchasing power of the wages of half of American fulltime jobs has barely increased.

This difference in the respective evolutions of the median wage and the mean wage reflects an increasing divergence in the rate of evolution of wages: the corollary of the fact that half of American wages grew more slowly than the mean is that the other half grew faster than the mean. In recent decades the gap between the lowest and the highest wages has continuously widened.

At the same time, the deep depression in activity, which had been impossible t o prevent or stem, drew attention to a new reality: the maintenance of full employment in an industrial economy is no simple matter. In the aftermath of the stock market crash, the number of unemployed did in fact rise dramatically and most American households, having seen the value of their savings melt away, found themselves facing the prospect of a miserable old age.

If the prosperity of all depends on each person's work, nothing must be allowed to discourage individual effort; on the contrary, what each receives must depend on his own work alone provided that work for all is to be found.

C) EQUAL DISTRIBUTION OF INCOME:

The "average individual" can be defined as the person in the middle of the global income distribution: the individual who receives the median level of income in the global Economy. One way of gauging the extent of global inequality is to compare the income of the average individual to average global income (that is, global gross domestic product [GDP] per capita). Where income is distributed evenly, median and average incomes would coincide. The more unequal the world economy is, the larger is the gap between the two. Global inequality is thus much higher than within-country inequality. Today, China's income distribution is centered at the middle of the global income distribution. The result is that the global Economy now has a much larger middle class, with Chinese households making up a large part of it.

Broadening the analysis to include the incomes Americans derive from their work and the incomes obtained from their financial or property wealth makes no difference to this conclusion.

Adjusted for the rise in consumer prices, the sum of these two components – personal income before transfers and taxes – received by American adults in the lower half of the income scale has shown no increase since the 1980s. This is hardly surprising: the distribution of wealth-income has shown even more inequality than has labor income and proceeded in a direction unfavorable to the lowest-paid workers.

In the end, it is only the impact of public redistribution that seems to have permitted some slight progress in real terms in the level of Americans' median disposable income. The taxes paid by those with remunerations in the bottom half of the scale have risen more slowly than the transfers they receive from the federal government.

Three conclusions can be drawn from recent evidence on the global distribution of income:

- The middle of the global income distribution has filled out in recent decades, thanks largely to China's rise.
- Differences across average incomes of countries remain the dominant force behind global inequality. ➢ Aggregate economic growth in the poorest countries is the most potent vehicle for reducing global inequality.
- The more rapid growth of developing countries since the 1990s is the key behind the recent decline in global inequality At the dawn of the Industrial Revolution, the gap between the richest and poorest parts of the world economy stood at a ratio of roughly 2:1; the between-country component of global inequality was minuscule. Today, the income gap between the richest and poorest economies of the world has risen to more than 80:1. What happened in between is that parts of the world economy Western Europe, the United States, Japan, and a few other countries took off while the rest of the world grew very slowly, when at all, often losing ground after temporary spurts.

Of the developed countries, it is the United States where the evolution in income distribution has been most spectacular, with the share of the top decline higher today than it was at the beginning of the twentieth century and the share of the 0.1% highest earners now larger than that of the 50% earning the least.

D) DOMESTIC AND FOREIGN DEBT:

Since the US dollar is the most widely used currency in global trade and financial transactions, US monetary policy and investor sentiment changes significantly influence global financing conditions.

The next collection of facts related to frontier growth look beyond the aggregate of GDP. These facts are related to structural change (the decline of agriculture and the rise of services, especially health), changes in leisure and fertility, rising inequality, and falling commodity prices.

Despite everything, the global economy is essential for the United States. Affiliates of US multinationals operating abroad and affiliates of foreign companies located in the United States account for a sizable share of output, employment, cross-border trade and financial flows. One-sixth of consumer goods purchases by US consumers are for imported goods, with an even higher share in Automobiles and consumer electronics.

The US dollar is the most widely used currency in international trade and financial markets and is the world's preeminent reserve currency. Around 80 percent of EMDE bond issuance and more than 50 percent of cross-border bank flows to EMDEs are denominated in US dollars.

Europe and Central Asia is the only EMDE region where the euro surpass the US dollar as the currency of denomination for cross-border bank flows. Ecuador, El Salvador, and Panama use the US dollar as their official currency; more than 30 other EMDEs maintain exchange rate pegs against the US dollar. A large share of official foreign exchange reserves 63 percent are dollar-denominated. The US dollar is widely used in international trade transactions for current account transactions, accounting for about one-third of invoicing goods and services in Europe and two-thirds in Asia. (Goldberg and Tille 2008, 2016; Devereux and Shi 2013).

Cheap money and a weak dollar also encouraged governments and corporations in emerging countries to borrow money, often denominated in US dollars. This increased both sovereign and private debt.

The United States has largely recovered from the worst financial crisis since the Great Depression and is performing well by several measures.

However, there are a number of serious challenges. As of 2015, US federal debt stood at 74 percent of gross domestic product, the eighth-highest ratio in history. Debt projections will hit 103 percent of gross domestic product (GDP) by 2040. (https://www.reuters.com/article/us-usa-budget/cbo-sees-u-s- deficitdoubling-by-2040-slower-interest-rate-rise-idUSKBN0OW1RY201 50616).

CHAPTER 4

IS THE US ECONOMY A MIXED
OR MARKET ECONOMY?

Each year, a quarter of the world's output is produced by a population accounting for less than 5% of the planet's total. The US government has always played a role in the economic affairs of the nation. Throughout its history, many services began to come under the influence or direct control of the public sector. The United States has a mixed economy. It works according to an economic system that features characteristics of both capitalism and socialism. A mixed economic system protects private property and allows a level of economic freedom in the use of capital and allows governments to intervene in economic activities to achieve social aims and the public good.

For more than a century now, the United States has led the way for the other industrialized countries. Not only has the trajectory of these other countries' GDP per head a crude but simple measure of an economy's level of development tracked that of the United States, but the structure of their activity has tended to converge with that of the American Economy. At the same time, they have emulated its modes of production and consumption. However, the social model associated with this pioneering role played by the United States has remained virtually unique. In very few other countries there has been such a reluctance to accept state intervention. The "flexibility" of the labor market has remained greater than in other countries.

Admittedly, the US economy is still one of the most productive, and in many sectors, its companies are the most innovative. For almost 40 years now, the continuous growth in economic activity has ceased to fuel social progress.

The standard of living of Americans occupying the lower half of the distribution of income has barely risen and inequalities in the distribution of income and wealth have reached a point at which the country's social and political equilibrium could at some stage be placed in jeopardy.

The American advance in economic development can also be seen in the convergence between the sectoral composition of activity in other industrialized economies and that seen in the United States. As the gap between their development levels and that of the United States narrowed, the importance of primary sectors (mining and agriculture) and manufacturing tended to decline. Private and public services rose, in each case tending towards American levels. The American primary sector, which accounted for 10% of GDP in 1950, was equivalent to no more than 5% from 1970 on, a proportion reached in European countries three decades later.

As for the proportion attained by the manufacturing industry, this too in all countries, except Germany and Japan, has fallen below 15% of GDP. These tendencies reflect a convergence between the other countries' modes of production and often also consumption and those of the United States.

Indeed, some of the most enduring debates of American economic history focus on the relative roles of the public and private sectors. This emphasis on private ownership arises, in part, from American beliefs about personal freedom. But there are limits to free enterprise, Whereas, Americans have always believed that some services are better performed by public rather than private enterprise.

The use of terms such as "political economy" and "social economy" is a signal that economic systems are closely intertwined with the institutions and activities of the government and society. It is important to note that capitalist economies are mixed economies because economic institutions do not stand alone, but rather interact. A main economic objective of the state covers the following areas:

➤

- economic freedom;
- economic effectiveness;
- economic justice;
- economic security;
- full employment;
- stable level of money;
- economic growth

- Economic freedom implies each country to ensure sufficient freedom of its economic agent's sellers and buyers, and they perform smoothly and efficiently their business.
- Economic efficiency requires any advanced society to strive for maximum economic efficiency, perceives it as a basis for their welfare.
- Economic justice presupposes a democratic country to seek economic justice because it recognizes that it is the basis for peace in society.
- Economic security, in turn, requires each country to seek to protect its citizens from economic risks (crises, bankruptcies, unemployment, accidents, etc.). By aid subsidies, state, etc. Full employment as an economic aim of the country requires every state to seek to provide economic Resources in production. Full employment of labor resources occur when everyone who can and wants to work finds a suitable job.

The other major social measures put in place by the federal government are more recent. These were introduced at another dramatic turning point in the Surviving in a Buoyant Economy country's history, when President Kennedy's assassination rocked American society to its foundations and blacks were granted their civil rights. When declaring his War on Poverty in his first State of the Union address in January1964, President Johnson stated: "Unfortunately, many Americans live on the outskirts of hope some because of their poverty and some because of their color, and all too many because of both." Alongside measures to provide immediate assistance, he announced others of a more long-term nature. The Elementary and Secondary Education Act was signed in 1965 and has been regularly renewed since then. This aimed to correct inequalities in the quality of the primary and secondary education received by children from low-income families.

It is a golden mixture of capitalism and socialism. Under this system there i s freedom of economic activities and government interferences for social welfare. Hence, it is a blend of both economies. The concept of mixed economy is of recent origin.

MAIN FEATURES OF MIXED ECONOMY:

(i.)   Co-existence of Private and Public Sector:
(ii.) Personal Freedom:
(iii.) Private Property is allowed:
(iv.) Economic Planning:
(v.)   Price Mechanism and Controlled Price:
(vi.) Profit Motive and Social Welfare:
(vii.) Check on Economic Inequalities:
(viii.)   Control of Monopoly Power:

TYPES OF MIXED ECONOMY:

1.)   Capitalistic Mixed Economy
2.)   Socialistic Mixed Economy
   a)   Liberal Socialistic Mixed Economy
   b)   Centralized Socialistic Mixed Economy A mixed economy is a system that combines characteristics of market, command, and traditional economies. It benefits from the advantages of all three while suffering from few of the disadvantages.

ADVANTAGES

- First, it distributes goods and services to where they are most needed.
- Second, it rewards the most efficient producers with the highest profit.
- Third, it encourages innovation to meet customer needs more creatively, cheaply or efficiently.
- Fourth, it automatically allocates capital to the most innovative and efficient producers.

DISADVANTAGES

- If the market has too much freedom, it can leave the less competitive members of society without any government support. However, central planning of government industries also creates problems.

CHAPTER 5

TAXES AND TARIFFS AND THEIR IMPACT ON THE US ECONOMY

A foreign national may be subject to one of two drastically different taxation systems by the United States depending on whether he is classified as a resident (expatriates) or a nonresident alien of the United States. The determination of residency status is critical. As a rule, classification as a nonresident foreign national may provide distinct tax advantages, but, in individual cases, the advantages of resident versus nonresident status may vary from year to year. Therefore, foreign nationals need to come to the United States annually to review the options available to minimize their tax liability in the United States and their home countries. Taxation of Foreign Nationals by the United States provides a basic overview of US taxes and how they affect foreign nationals. (Taxation of foreign nationals by the US 2016) A)

TAX:

The term Taxation is the imposition of compulsory levies on individuals or entities by governments. Taxes are levied in almost every country of the world, primarily to raise revenue for government expenditures, although they serve other purposes.

In the OECD classification, the term "taxes" is confined to compulsory, unrequited payments to the general government. Taxes are unrequited because the government's benefits to taxpayers are not normally in proportion to their payments.

The term "tax" does not include fines unrelated to tax offenses and compulsory loans paid to the government. Borderline cases between tax and nontax revenues concerning certain charges. The general government consists of supra-national authorities, the central administration, and the agencies whose operations are under its effective control, state and local governments and their administrations, social security schemes, and autonomous governmental entities, excluding public enterprises. Apart from the reference to supra-national authorities, this definition of government follows that of the "System of National Accounts" (SNA), United Nations 1968.

Compulsory payments to supra-national bodies, such as the Commission of the European Communities and their agencies, are included like taxes and are treated as part of the country's tax revenues in which they are collected. They are separately identified in the data on subsectors of government. In countries where the church forms part of the general government, church taxes are included, provided they meet the criteria set out in the paragraph above. This may be true in other countries; moreover, when it comes to churches in the US under American tax law, churches are exempt from paying federal, state, and local taxes.

The general government receipts, levies paid to non-government bodies, welfare agencies, or social insurance schemes outside general government, trade unions, or trade associations, even where such levies are compulsory, are excluded. However, compulsory payments to the general government earmarked for such bodies are included provided that the government is not simply acting in an agency capacity.

Profits from fiscal monopolies are distinguished from those of other public enterprises. They are treated as taxes because they reflect the state's taxing power by using monopoly powers, as are profits received by the government from the purchase and sale of foreign exchange at different.

Taxes paid by governments (e.g., social security contributions and payroll taxes paid by governments in their capacity as an employer, consumption taxes on their purchases, or taxes on their property) are not excluded from the data provided. Despite everything, where it is possible to identify the amounts of revenue involved, they are shown in a memorandum item.

The relationship between this classification and SNA is set out in Section E. Because of the differences between the two classifications, the data shown in national accounts are sometimes calculated or classified differently from the practice set out in this book. These and other differences are mentioned where appropriate, but it is not possible to refer to all of them; there may also be some differences between this classification and that of being employed domestically by particular national administrations, so that OECD and national statistics data may not always be consistent; any such differences, however, are likely to be very slight in terms of amounts of revenues involved.

SOCIAL SECURITY CONTRIBUTIONS:

Compulsory social security contributions paid to the general government are treated as tax revenues. Being compulsory payments to the general government, they resemble taxes. They may, however, differ from taxes in that the receipt of social security benefits depends, in most countries, upon appropriate contributions having been made, although the size of the benefits is not necessarily related to the amount of the contributions. Better comparability between countries is obtained by treating social security contributions as taxes, but they are listed under a separate heading to be distinguished in any analysis. Social security contributions that are either voluntary or not payable to the general government are not treated as taxes. As indicated in the country footnotes, there are difficulties in eliminating voluntary contributions and compulsory payments to the private sector charges and license fees.

Apart from vehicle license fees, which are universally regarded as taxes, it is not easy to distinguish between those fees and user charges which are to be treated as taxes and those which are not, since, while a fee or charge is levied in connection with a specific service or activity, the strength of the link between the fee and the service provided may vary considerably, as may the relation between the amount of levy and the cost of providing the service. Where the recipient of a service pays a fee related to the cost of providing the service, the levy may be regarded as requited and, under the definition, would not be considered as a tax.

In the following cases, a levy could be considered as "unrequited":

a)   Where the charge dramatically exceeds the cost of providing the service;

b)   Where the payer of the levy is not the receiver of the benefit (e.g., a fee collected from slaughterhouses to finance a service which is provided to farmers);

c)   Where the government is not providing a specific service in return for the levy which it receives even though a license may be issued to the payer (e.g., where the government grants hunting, fishing, or shooting license which is not accompanied by the right to use a specific area of government land);

d)   Where benefits are received only by those paying the levy, but the benefits received by each individual are not necessarily in proportion to his payments (e.g., a milk marketing levy paid by dairy farmers and used to promote the consumption of milk).

In marginal cases, the application of the criteria set out in paragraph 1 can b e particularly difficult. The solution adopted given the desirability of international uniformity and the relatively small amounts of revenue usually involved is to follow the predominant practice among tax administrations rather than allow each country to adopt its own view of whether such levies a r e regarded as taxes as non-tax revenue. A list of the main charges in question and their standard treatment in this bulletin is as follows: Non-tax revenues: court fees; driving license fees; harbor fees; passport fees; radio and television license fees where public authorities provide the service.

Taxes Of 5200: permission to perform such activities as distributing films; hunting, fishing, and shooting; providing entertainment or gambling facilities; selling alcohol or tobacco; permission to own dogs or to use or

OWN MOTOR VEHICLES OR GUNS; SEVE; ANCE TAXES:

In practice, it may not always be possible to isolate tax receipts from nontax revenue receipts when they are recorded together. If it is estimated that the bulk of the receipts derive from non-tax revenues, the whole is treated as non-tax revenue; otherwise, they are included and classified according to the rules.

Two differences between the OECD classification and SNA regarding the borderline between tax and non-tax revenues are:

a)   SNA classifies several levies as indirect taxes if paid by enterprises, but as non-tax revenues, if paid by households, a distinction which is regarded as irrelevant in this classification for distinguishing between tax and non-tax revenues.

b)   Predominant practice among most OECD tax administrations, which is occasionally used in this classification for distinguishing between tax and non-tax revenues, is not a relevant criterion for SNA purposes.

ROYALTIES:

Royalty payments for the right to extract oil and gas or to exploit other mineral resources are generally regarded as non-tax revenues since they are property income from government-owned land or resources.

Fines and penalties: Receipts from fines and penalties paid for infringement of regulations identified as relating to a particular tax and interest on payments overdue regarding a particular tax are recorded together with receipts from that tax. Other kinds of fines identifiable as relating to tax offenses are classified in the residual heading 6000. Fines not relating to tax offenses (e.g., for parking offenses) or not identifiable as relating to tax offenses are not treated as taxes.

RESIDENT ALIENS

The rules defining residency for US income tax purposes are particular, with only limited exceptions once the objective criteria or mechanical tests are met. Individuals classified as resident aliens are taxed on their worldwide income derived from any source. Tax rates are graduated, and income is determined in the same manner as for US citizens. Various elections may be available in the first year of residency to reduce the US tax liability.

NONRESIDENT ALIENS

Nonresident aliens usually are taxed only on income derived from US sources. US-source income that is considered "effectively connected" with a US trade or business, such as salary and other forms of compensation, is taxed at graduated rates. Taxable income from US trade or business entities can include some kinds of foreign source income and US-source income. US investment income is generally taxed at a flat 30% tax rate, which a tax treaty may reduce. Certain types of investment income may be exempt from US tax.

TAX TREATIES

For many nonresident aliens, the burden of US tax is reduced by tax treaties between the United States and their home countries. Further, treaties may modify US income taxation (for example, in determining residency status) and should be reviewed in every tax-planning situation involving a foreign national. Foreign investment in real property US real property can be a secure, diversified investment for foreign nationals. Many real estate investments in personal residences are converted into rental properties, and special rules apply to their treatment. Depreciation rules (relating to property placed in service after 1998) increase the period over which deductions are spread.

OTHER TAXES

In addition to federal income tax, foreign nationals may be subject to social security and estate, gift, and state taxes. These should all be considered in evaluating the tax effects of a US assignment. Tax planning Timing of income recognition and the length of an assignment can significantly affect a foreign national's US tax liability. Also, the tax basis (tax cost) of assets may not be computed for US tax purposes in the same way as in the foreign national's home country.

IMMIGRATION, VISA, AND NATIONALITY CONSIDERATIONS

Those who want to be employed in the United States must obtain visas to do s o . Most visas allowing employment in the United States require US Citizenship and Immigration Services (USCIS) approval before visa issuance at US consular posts abroad. Additionally, a valid Visa authorizing employment in the US, rather than merely allowing an alien individual to reside in the US, also authorizes the individual to receive a social security number (SSN). Nonresident and resident aliens who are not eligible for SSNs must apply for a taxpayer identification number following IRS prescribed procedures.

RESIDENT ALIEN DEFINED

A resident alien of the United States is a foreign national who meets either of two objective tests: the lawful permanent residence test or the substantial presence test. An alien who meets neither test is a nonresident alien for federal income tax purposes for that year. (The residence test is different for federal estate and gift tax purposes, and certain states may impose their own residency rules.) Under the lawful permanent residence test (also known as the green card test), an individual is considered a resident alien from the day that he/she is admitted to the United States as a lawful permanent resident (that is, given a "green card") until the day that this status is officially revoked or judicially found to be abandoned. While the alien officially has lawful permanent resident status, he/she is considered a US tax resident even while living outside the United States.

Under the substantial presence test, an individual must meet the following conditions to be considered a resident alien:
➤
- He/she must be physically present in the United States for thirty-one days in the current year, and
- He/she must be physically present in the United States for a weighted average of 183 days over a three-year testing period that comprises the current and the two preceding years. Days of US presence are computed under a weighting formula that counts the following days of presence: – All days in the current year – One-third of the days in the preceding year – One-sixth of the days in the second preceding year.

Exempt individuals may exclude some days from this calculation. The weighting formula permits an alien to spend up to 121 days each year in the United States without becoming an income tax resident. Also, the alien will not be considered a US resident for any year in which he/she has been present in the United States for fewer than thirty-one days.

EXEMPT INDIVIDUALS:

Exempt individuals are not legally "present" in the United States, even though they may be physically located there. These individuals are:

- Employees of foreign governments
- Teachers or trainees with J visas

- Students with F and J visas
- Professional athletes compete in charitable (as opposed to commercial) sports events, but only during actual competition. Except for professional athletes, the exempt status of an individual also applies to members of his/her immediate family.

TAXATION OF RESIDENT ALIENS:

Income subject to taxation:

All income received by a US resident alien or US citizen, derived from any source, is subject to federal income tax unless specifically exempt or excluded. A resident alien is taxed at graduated rates after allowance for deductions. Income comprises salary and allowances, moving expense reimbursements, dividends, interest, and gains from selling property, and other income from any source. For example, income received by the resident alien employee for services performed on temporary business trips overseas (outside the United States) is subject to US taxation. (A foreign tax credit may be allowed as an offset against the US tax liability if the individual also pays non-US taxes on this income.)

For individual income tax purposes, income generally refers to cash or the fair market value of property or services received by or made available to the individual. The appreciation in the value of investments or of other property is not income until the property is sold or exchanged for other property.

DEEMED INCOME

US tax law contains several provisions less commonly found in other countries' tax laws, deeming US investors to have received income earned by foreign corporations that they control, by passive foreign investment companies, and b y trusts that they have established for the benefit of US persons. These provisions apply entirely to resident aliens, and while these provisions tend to affect few resident aliens, their tax consequences can be surprising. These rules must therefore be considered carefully in evaluating US income tax status.

FOREIGN TAX CREDIT:

Income taxes paid by a resident alien to a foreign country may be deducted as an itemized deduction or may be credited against the resident alien's US tax liability. Since claiming foreign taxes as credits reduce US tax liability on a dollar-for-dollar basis, it will generally produce a lower net tax liability than claim an itemized deduction. An intricate series of limitations apply to the foreign tax credit. Foreign taxes paid on one type of income cannot be used as credits against US tax on other types of income. Any unused credits may be carried back for one year and forward for ten years to reduce US tax incurred on non-US income.

TAX TREATIES:

The United States has negotiated tax treaties with other countries to reduce the burden of double taxation. A treaty may override the income tax laws of the United States for items covered by the treaty. Any item not explicitly addressed by the treaty will be taxed following US income tax laws. Generally, treaties do not change the US taxation of a US citizen or resident. However, treaties may specifically define or modify residency status for purposes of the tax rules in the treaty. In general, an individual is considered a resident in the country in which he/she is subject to taxation. In some situations, that individual may be considered a resident by both treaty countries under their domestic laws. Many treaties include tiebreaker rules to determine the country of residence for treaty purposes. The tiebreaker rules override the domestic laws of each country. They are based on such factors as the location of the individual's permanent home and his/her economic and personal relationships. Individuals who are considered US resident aliens under either the green card or substantial presence test may use treaties to reduce US taxation.

For example, a green card holder living abroad and qualifying as a resident of the treaty country under the tiebreaker rule of the treaty may qualify for a US tax exemption or reduction to the extent provided in the treaty. Well!!! The treaties can be used to reduce

US taxation only in specific situations. Green card holders are cautioned that filing Form 1040NR (the nonresident return) with a disclosure statement claiming residence in a foreign treaty country could adversely affect their continuing qualification for the green card. Dual-resident foreign nationals claiming treaty benefits must file Form 1040NR as nonresident aliens concerning that portion of the tax year for which they were considered nonresident. The return must contain Form 8833, Treaty-Based Return Position Disclosure Under Section 6114 or 7701(b) of Taxation of Foreign Nationals by US 2016.

Penalties could apply for failure to file this form or a similar statement. An individual who is a US resident under a treaty may also use the treaty's rules to reduce taxation in the other country when appropriate. For example, a US resident alien may be able to claim a reduced withholding tax rate on interest and dividend income generated in his/her home country, provided that he/she is deemed to be a US resident under the treaty between the United States and the home country income tax of treaty countries.

TAXATION OF NONRESIDENT ALIENS:

Nonresident aliens are taxed separately on income from US sources that are n o t effectively connected with a US trade or business (for example, investment income) and on income effectively connected with a US trade or business (for example, business and compensation income). Generally, the Surviving in a Buoyant Economy source of income is the geographic location where the related services are performed and where the income-producing asset is located. The nonresident alien tax base is compared to the resident alien tax base.

A) ATTRIBUTES OF A GOOD TAX (CANONS OF TAXATION):

By canons of taxation, we simply mean the characteristics or qualities of a sound tax system. Canons of taxation are related to the administrative part of a tax. Adam Smith first devised the principles or canons of taxation in 1776 in his famous book 'The Wealth of Nations.

Even in the twenty-first century, the modern governments applied Smithian canons of taxation while imposing and collecting taxes.

These canons of taxation define numerous rules and principles upon which a good taxation system should be built. Although these canons of taxation were presented a very long time ago, they are still used as the foundation of discussion on the principles of taxation.

Adam Smith initially presented only four canons of taxation, commonly referred to as the 'Main Canons of Taxation' or 'Adam Smith's Canons of Taxation. Along with overtime, more canons were developed to suit the modern economies better. In the following article, you will read the nine canons of taxation most commonly discussed and used.

Adam Smith's Canons of Taxation: Adam Smith initially presented the following four canons of taxation.

The rest were developed later:

1.) Canon of Equality
2.) Canon of Certainty
3.) Canon of Convenience
4.) Canon of Economy

These nine canons of taxation are:

1.) Canon of Equality
2.) Canon of Certainty
3.) Canon of Convenience
4.) Canon of Economy
5.) Canon of Productivity
6.) Canon of Simplicity
7.) Canon of Diversity
8.) Canon of Elasticity
9.) Canon of Flexibility

B) TARIFF:

Income not effectively connected with a US trade or business. A nonresident alien's US-source income that is not effectively connected with a US trade or business is subject to tax at the flat rate of 30% of gross income; no deductions are allowed. Treaties may reduce this flat rate. Income subject to this 30% tax includes interest, dividends, royalties, rents, and other fixed or determinable annual or periodic income. An exception is provided for portfolio income on certain US-registered bonds and bank accounts. This interest is not taxed unless it is effectively connected with a US trade or business.

When to file Tax returns for individuals is due on the fifteenth day of the fourth month following the close of the tax year (15 April for calendar year taxpayers). An additional automatic extension of six months, to 15 October, is available by filing Form 4868, Application for Automatic Extension of Time to File US Individual Income Tax Return. This extension provides additional time to file the income tax return; however, it does not extend the date to pay any tax owed. Interest will accrue on any amount owed until the tax liability has been paid. If the due date for filing a return (including the automatic extension)

Falls on a Saturday, Sunday, or national holiday, the due date is deferred to the next earliest business day. A return is considered filed on time if an official postmark (the US or foreign postmark is accepted) dated on or before the last day for filing, including extensions. Similarly, returns filed through an IRS-designated private delivery service are also considered filed on the date mailed. Tax returns filed by a private delivery service which is not an IRS-designated private delivery service, must reach the IRS office by the required due date. See Appendix A for a list of currently designated private delivery services. If a return is mailed after its original or extended due date, it is not considered filed until received by the IRS. Interest and penalties on balance due A properly filed extension relieve the taxpayer from a late filing penalty on the net tax due (4.5% per month for late filing plus .5% per month for late payment until the payment is made; the combined penalties may not exceed 25%). However, it does not eliminate the liability for interest charged on any unpaid tax from the original due date (without extension). Example: Taxpayer B is living in the US as of 15 April 2002. On 10 April 2002, he files a valid Form 4868 extension for his 20X1 US income tax return. He then files the return on 15 September 2002,and there is a $1,000 balance due. Because B filed his return before the 15 October extended due date, no late filing penalty was assessed. He will be subject to the late payment penalty and interest charges, calculated as follows (assume a 3% annual interest rate): Late payment penalty: 0.5% x 5 months x $1,000 = $25 5 months counted from 15 April to 15 September Interest: 3% x 154 days/365 days x $1,000 = $13 154 days counted from 15 April to 15 September.

Estimated tax: Estimated tax payments are required if the total tax amount due with the return after withholding is expected to exceed $1,000.

Taxpayer identification numbers Regardless of US income tax residency status, an individual must have a valid US Social Security Number (SSN), or valid Individual Taxpayer Identification Number (ITIN) to file a US income tax return.

SALE OF PROPERTY BY RESIDENT ALIENS

The gain or loss on the sale of residential rental property is the difference between the net selling price (sales price fewer expenses of sale) and the property's adjusted basis. A property's adjusted basis is its original cost less the total amount of depreciation expenses claimed during its life.

SALE OF PROPERTY BY NONRESIDENT ALIENS

In general, a gain or loss from a sale or other disposition of US real property interests (USRPIs) by a nonresident alien is treated as if it were effectively connected with a trade or business within the United States, regardless of the property's actual use. All nonresident alien individuals, regardless of whether they engaged in a trade or business or elected to treat real property income as effectively connected with a trade or business, will be treated alike when taxed on gains from real property sales.

Any gain from the disposition of a USRPI will be taxed at the graduated rates, limited to a maximum tax of 15% or 20% if the USRPI is a capital asset and the gain is long-term. The higher 20% maximum tax rate applies to individuals falling in the highest graduated income tax bracket (i.e., 39.6%). As with resident aliens, losses can be offset against gains only if the property was used in a business or income-producing property; personal-use property does not generate a deductible loss. Upon purchasing a USRPI from a nonresident alien, the purchaser may be required to withhold 10% of the proceeds, to be applied against the seller's tax on the gain. The IRS may agree to lower the withholding rate if the expected tax would be less than the otherwise required 10%. Withholding does not apply if the sale or exchange falls within a few narrowly defined tax-free exchanges (although reporting may be required) or if the purchaser acquires the property for use as his or her residence. The purchase price does not exceed $300,000.

NET INVESTMENT INCOME TAX

For tax years beginning after December 31, 2012, certain US taxpayers may b e subject to an additional net investment income tax (NII). The tax is in addition to regular federal income tax and intended to reach certain higher- income taxpayers' unearned income. Nonresident aliens, including those who Surviving in a Buoyant Economy, assert nonresident US tax status under an income tax treaty are not subject to NII. Dual status resident taxpayers are subject to NII only concerning the portion of their residency period of the dual-status tax year. For individuals subject to tax on NII, tax is imposed at 3.8% on the lesser of

- the individual's net investment income for the tax year, or
- the excess of the individual's Modified Adjusted Gross Income over the threshold amount (the MAGI threshold amount is $250,000 for individuals filing a joint return,

$125,000 for married taxpayers filing a separate return and $200,000 for all other individuals).

An individual's Net Investment Income includes three general categories of income:

1.) Gross income from interest, dividends, annuities, rents, and royalties;
2.) Income derived from a passive activity or a trade or business of trading financial instruments or commodities; and
3.) Net gain recognized on dispositions of property.

State and local income taxes almost all of the fifty states, the District of Columbia, and even some cities levy some form of personal income tax that is separate and distinct from the income tax imposed by the federal government. The tax base may be broader or narrower than that used by the federal government. California's "unitary" tax is a well-known example of a broad tax base. On the other hand, New Hampshire and Tennessee states have personal income taxes but apply them only to passive investment income (that is, interest, dividends, and capital gains). State income taxes are independent of each other as well as of the federal tax. This can lead to double or even multiple state taxation of the same income. Double taxation is usually prevented by a credit, which is allowed on the tax return of the state of residence for taxes paid to the state that is the source of income. State income taxes are generally levied on the worldwide taxable income of residents of the state. For nonresidents, they are levied on income from sources within the state.

THE NEED FOR TAX PLANNING

Various actions that resident and nonresident aliens take can affect the tax they will pay in the United States. Tax planning, therefore, is essential for foreign nationals who are or will become subject to taxation by the United States.

TIMING OF INCOME RECOGNITION

Foreign nationals are subject to standard US accounting rules. They recognize income in the amounts and at times prescribed in US tax law, even though this income may pertain to activity with no US connection. For example, income earned by a cash-basis taxpayer before becoming a resident but received by him/her after becoming a resident will be subject to US income tax in the year received.

Tax treaties Some of the more commonly used treaty benefits are

- Tax exemption for compensation earned under certain dollar limits or during limited periods
- Lower rates of withholding for interest and dividend income
- Exemption from social security withholding (under social security totalization agreements)
- Preferential treatment for capital gains and pension income. Foreign investments Foreign investors should have their investments carefully reviewed as part of the tax-planning process before starting a US assignment. Some ideas to consider are as follows:
- Foreign trusts, of which the nonresident alien is a beneficiary, may choose t o distribute current and (especially) accumulated income before the beneficiary becomes a resident alien. (The United States imposes a disadvantageous tax regime on distributions of accumulated income from foreign trusts.)
- Foreign corporations controlled by a nonresident alien may choose to pay out dividends before the nonresident establishes US residency. Dividends paid out while the individual is considered a nonresident are not subject to US taxation. In addition, the corporation will have reduced its accumulated earnings and profits, which could favorably affect the later income tax treatment.

PERMANENT ESTABLISHMENT:

1.) For this Convention, the term "permanent establishment" means a fixed place of business through which the business of an enterprise is wholly or partly carried on.

2.) The term "permanent establishment" includes especially:
   a) **a place of management;**
   b) **a branch;**
   c) **an office;**
   d) **a factory;**
   e) **a workshop;**
   f) **a mine, an oil or gas well, a quarry, or any other place of extraction of natural resources.**

3.) A building site or construction or installation project, or an installation or drilling rig or ship used for the exploration or exploitation of the sea bed and its subsoil and their natural resources, situated in one of the Contracting States constitutes a permanent establishment only if it lasts, or the activities of the rig or ship last, for more than twelve months. For the sole purpose of determining whether the twelve-month period referred to in this paragraph has been exceeded:
   a) where an enterprise of a Contracting State carries on activities in the other Contracting State at a place that constitutes a building site or construction or installation project, and these activities are carried on during periods that in the aggregate do not last more than twelve months;
   b) connected activities are carried on at the same building site or construction or installation project during different periods, each exceeding thirty days, by one or more enterprises that are connected persons concerning the first-mentioned enterprise, these different periods shall be added to the periods during which the first-mentioned enterprise has carried on activities at that building site or construction or installation project.

4.) Not withstanding the preceding provisions of this Article, the term "permanent establishment" shall be deemed not to include:

    a) The use of facilities solely for storage, display, or delivery of goods or merchandise belonging to the enterprise;

    b) The maintenance of a stock of goods or merchandise belonging to the enterprise solely for storage, display, or delivery;

    c) The maintenance of a stock of goods or merchandise belonging to the enterprise solely for processing by another enterprise;

    d) The maintenance of a fixed place of business solely to purchase goods or merchandise, or of collecting information, for the enterprise;

    e) The maintenance of a fixed place of business solely to carry on, for t h e enterprise, any other activity of a preparatory or auxiliary character;

    f) The maintenance of a fixed place of business solely for any combination of the activities mentioned in subparagraphs that enterprise shall be deemed to have a permanent establishment in that Contracting State

5.) An enterprise shall not be deemed to have a permanent establishment in a Contracting State merely because it carries on business in that Contracting State through a broker, general commission agent, or any other agent of an independent status, provided that such persons are acting in the ordinary course of their business as independent agents.

6.) The fact that a company that is a resident of a Contracting State controls or is controlled by a company that is a resident of the other Contracting State, or that carries on business in that other Contracting State (whether through a permanent establishment or otherwise), shall not be taken into account in determining whether either company has a permanent establishment in that other Contracting State.

BUSINESS PROFITS

1.) Profits of a Contracting State enterprise shall be taxable only in that Contracting State unless the enterprise carries on business in the other Contracting State through a permanent establishment situated therein. If the enterprise carries on business as aforesaid, the profits are attributable t o the permanent establishment following the provisions of other Contracting State.

2.) For this Article, the profits that are attributable in each Contracting State to the permanent establishment referred to in paragraph 1 of this Article are the profits it might be expected to make, in particular in its dealings with other parts of the enterprise, if it were a separate and independent enterprise engaged in the same or similar activities under the same or similar conditions, taking into account the functions performed, assets used and risks assumed by the enterprise through the permanent establishment and the other parts of the enterprise.

3.) Where, following paragraph 2 of this Article, a Contracting State adjusts the profits that are attributable to a permanent establishment of an enterprise of one of the Contracting States and taxes accordingly profits of the enterprise that have been charged to tax in the other Contracting State, the other Contracting State shall, to the extent necessary to eliminate double taxation, make an appropriate adjustment if it agrees with the adjustment made by the first-mentioned Contracting State; if the other Contracting State does not so agree, the Contracting States shall eliminate any double taxation resulting from that place by mutual agreement.

4.) Where profits include items of income that are dealt with separately in other Articles of this Convention, then the provisions of those Articles shall not be affected by the provisions of this Article.

5.) In applying this Article, paragraph 8 of Article 10 (Dividends), paragraph 5 of Article 11 (Interest), paragraph 5 of Article 12 (Royalties), paragraph 3 of Article 13 (Gains), and paragraph 3 of Article 21 (Other Income), any income, profit or gain attributable to a permanent establishment during its existence is taxable in the Contracting State where such permanent establishment is situated even if the payments are deferred until such permanent establishment has ceased to exist.

SHIPPING AND AIR TRANSPORT

1.) Profits of a Contracting State enterprise from the operation of ships or aircraft in international traffic shall be taxable only in that Contracting State.

2.) For purposes of this Article, profits from the operation of ships or aircraft include, but are not limited to:

a) profits from the rental of ships or aircraft on a full (time or voyage) basis;

b) Profits from the rental on a bareboat basis of ships or aircraft if the rental income is incidental to profits from the operation of ships or aircraft in international traffic; and

c) Profits from the rental on a bareboat basis of ships or aircraft if such ships or aircraft are operated in international traffic by the lessee. Profits derived by an enterprise from the inland transport of property or passengers within either Contracting State shall be treated as profits from the operation of ships or aircraft in international traffic if such transport is undertaken as part of international traffic.

3.) Profits of an enterprise of a Contracting State from the use, maintenance, or rental of containers (including trailers, barges, and related equipment for the transport of containers) shall be taxable only in that Contracting

State, except to the extent that those containers are used for transport solely between places within the other Contracting State.

4.) The provisions of paragraphs 1 and 3 of this Article shall also apply to profits from participating in a pool, a joint business, or an international operating agency.

ASSOCIATED ENTERPRISES:

Where:

a) An enterprise of a Contracting State participates directly or indirectly i n the management, control, or capital of an enterprise of the other Contracting State; or

b) the same persons participate directly or indirectly in the management, control, or capital of an enterprise of a Contracting State and an enterprise of the other Contracting State. In either case, conditions are made or imposed between the two enterprises in their commercial or financial relations that differ from those made between independent enterprises. Any profits that, but for those conditions, would have accrued to one of the enterprises, but because of those conditions have not so accrued, may be included in the profits of that enterprise and taxed accordingly.

2. Where a Contracting State includes in the profits of an enterprise of that Contracting State, and taxed accordingly, profits on which an enterprise of the other Contracting State has been charged to tax in that other Contracting State. The other Contracting State agrees that the profits so included are profits that would have accrued to the enterprise of the first- mentioned Contracting State if the conditions made between the two enterprises had been those that would have been made between independent enterprises, then that other Contracting State shall make an appropriate adjustment to the amount of the tax charged therein on those profits. In determining such

adjustment, due regard shall be had to the other provisions of this Convention, and the competent authorities of the Contracting States shall, if necessary, consult each other.

DIVIDENDS

1.) Dividends paid by a company that is a resident of a Contracting State to a resident of the other Contracting State may be taxed in that other Contracting State.

2.) Anyway, such dividends may also be taxed in the Contracting State of which the company paying the dividends is a resident and according to the laws of that Contracting State, but if the beneficial owner of the dividends is a resident of the other Contracting State, except as otherwise provided, the tax so charged shall not exceed:

   a)   5 percent of the gross amount of the dividends if, for the twelvemonth period ending on the date on which the entitlement to the dividends is determined:

   (i.)   The beneficial owner has been a company that was a resident of the other Contracting State or a third qualifying state. The term "qualifying third state" means a state that has in effect a comprehensive convention for the avoidance of double taxation with the Contracting State of the company paying the dividends that would have allowed the beneficial owner to benefit from a rate of tax on dividends that is less than or equal to 5 percent; and

   (ii.)   At least 10 percent of the aggregate vote and value of the shares of the payer of the dividends was owned directly by the beneficial owner or a qualifying predecessor owner. The term "qualifying predecessor owner" means a company from which the beneficial owner acquired the shares of the payer of the dividends, but only if such company was, at the time the shares were acquired, a connected person concerning the beneficial owner of the dividend, and a resident of a state that has in effect a comprehensive convention for the avoidance of double taxation with the Contracting State of the company paying the dividends that would have allowed such company to benefit from a rate of tax on dividends that is less than or equal to 5 percent. For this purpose, a company that is a resident of a Contracting State shall be considered to own directly the shares owned by an entity that:

A) Is considered fiscally transparent under the laws of that Contracting State; and

B) Is not a resident of the other Contracting State of which the company paying the dividends is a resident; in proportion to the company's ownership interest in that entity; and 19

b) 15 percent of the gross amount of the dividends in all other cases. This paragraph shall not affect the taxation of the company in respect of the profits out of which the dividends are paid.

3.) Not withstanding the provisions of paragraph 2 of this Article, dividends shall not be taxed in the Contracting State of which the company paying the dividends is a resident if:

a) The beneficial owner of the dividends is a pension fund that is a resident of the other Contracting State;

b) Such dividends are not derived from the carrying on of a trade or business by the pension fund or through a person that is a connected person concerning the pension fund.

I) TYPES OF TARIFF:

Tariffs restrict imports by increasing the price of goods and services purchased from another country, making them less attractive to domestic consumers. There are two types of tariffs: A specific tariff is levied as a fixed fee based on the type of item, such as a $1,000 tariff on a car. An ad-valorem tariff is levied based on the item's value, such as 10% of the value of the vehicle.

C) IMPACT OF TAX AND TARIFF ON US ECONOMY:

In March 2018, President Trump began to impose a series of tariffs and, later, quotas on selected US steel and aluminum imports from several countries under Section 232 of the Trade Expansion Act of 1962. In addition, on July 6, 2018, President Trump applied the first in a series of tariffs on imports of selected products imported from China, in retaliation for China's refusal to change intellectual property rights-related acts, policies, and practices that the Office of the US Trade Representative (USTR) had determined were adversely affecting US companies. In each instance, US trading partners retaliated with tariffs of their own, applied to a range of US exports. As of November 1, 2018, US tariffs affected $255 billion in US imports, and foreign retaliatory tariffs were being applied to $124 billion in US exports.

The President has also threatened to impose additional tariffs on imports of motor vehicles and parts but has agreed to remove certain suppliers from coverage, at least for now. The total value of the potentially affected motor vehicle and parts trade is $28 billion, with commensurate retaliation to US exports.

The President has threatened to impose tariffs on the balance of US imports from China if China continues to fail to implement a long list of changes to i ts intellectual property rights policies and practices and narrow its trade surplus with the United States. China has again threatened to retaliate in kind. These threatened tariffs would affect an additional $290 billion in US imports, with commensurate retaliation to US exports.

The escalation of tariffs, both by the United States and by US trading partners, impacts US producers and consumers and, as a consequence, US workers. Some of those effects are positive (increased production and output in sectors protected by the tariffs); others are negative (higher costs to consumers – both US manufacturers and households – who must pay the tariffs.

I) GROSS DOMESTIC PRODUCT/ GROSS NET PRODUCT:

Gross national product (GNP) is the value of all goods and services made by a country's residents and businesses, regardless of production location. GNP counts the investments made by US residents and businesses both inside and outside the country and computes the value of all products manufactured by domestic companies, regardless of where they are made.

GNP doesn't count any income earned in the United States by foreign residents or businesses and excludes products manufactured in the United States by overseas firms.

2019 compared to the previous quarter. This rate is the same as in the previous quarter.

The year-on-year change in GDP was 2.1%, 1 -tenth of one percent more than the 2% recorded Gross Domestic Product of United States grew 0.5% in the third quarter of in the second quarter of 2019.

The GDP figure in the third quarter of 2019 was $5,385,635 million; United States is the world's leading economy about GDP, as can be seen in the ranking of quarterly GDP of the 50 countries that we publish. United States has a quarterly GDP per capita of $14,796, $1084 higher than the same quarter last year.

According to their GDP per capita, if we order the countries according to their GDP per capita, United States is in 6th position of the 50 countries.

GNP VS. GDP

US GNP says a lot about the financial well-being of Americans and US-based multinational corporations, but it doesn't give much insight into the health of the US economy. For that, you should use gross domestic product (real or nominal) measures production inside of a country, no matter who makes it. GNP is the same as GDP + Z.

That means GNP is a more accurate measure of a country's income than its production.

EXAMPLES OF GNP VS. GDP

The output of a Toyota plant in Kentucky isn't included in GNP. However, it's counted in GDP because the revenue from the sales of Toyota vehicles goes to Japan, even though the products are made and sold in the United States. It is included in GDP because it adds to the health of the US economy by creating jobs for Kentucky residents, who use their wages to buy local goods and services.

D) GROSS DOMESTIC PRODUCT:

GDP measures the monetary value of final goods and services, those bought by the final user produced in a country in a given period (say a quarter or a year). It counts all of the output generated within the borders of a country. GDP is composed of goods and services produced for sale in the market and includes some nonmarket production, such as defense or education services provided by the government. Theoretically, GDP can be viewed in three different ways:

- the production approach sums the "value-added" at each stage of production, where value-added is defined as total sales less the value of intermediate inputs into the production process.
- The expenditure approach adds up the value of purchases made by final users, for example, the consumption of food, televisions, and medical services by households; the investments in machinery by companies; and the purchases of goods and services by the government and foreigners.
- The income approach sums the incomes generated by production, for example, the compensation employees receive and the operating surplus of companies (roughly sales fewer costs).

GDP in a country is usually calculated by the national statistical agency, which compiles the information from many sources. In making the calculations, however, most countries follow established international standards.

E) GROSS NATIONAL PRODUCT:

Gross national product (GNP) estimates the total value of all the final products and services turned out in a given period utilizing production owned by a country's residents. GNP is commonly calculated by taking the sum of p e r s o n a l consumption expenditures, private domestic investment, government expenditure, net exports, and any income earned by residents from overseas investments, minus income earned within the domestic economy by foreign residents. Net exports represent the difference between what a country exports minus any imports of goods and services.

GNP is related to another crucial economic measure called gross domestic product (GDP), which considers all output produced within a country's borders regardless of who owns the means of production. GNP starts with GDP, adds residents' investment income from overseas investments, and subtracts foreign residents' investment income earned within a country.

F) FACTORS THAT INFLUENCE US GDP/GNP:

1. Poor health and low levels of education
People who don't have access to healthcare or education have lower levels of productivity. This lack of access means the labor force is not as productive as it could be. Therefore, the economy does not reach the productivity it could have otherwise.

2. Lack of necessary infrastructure
Developing nations often suffer from inadequate infrastructures such as roads, schools, and hospitals. This lack of infrastructure makes transportation more expensive and slows the overall efficiency of the country.

3. Flight of Capital

If the country does not deliver the returns expected from investors, investors will pull out their money. Money often flows out of the country to seek higher rates of returns.

4. Political Instability

Similarly, political instability in the government scares investors and hinders investment. For example, historically, Zimbabwe had been plagued with political uncertainty and laws favoring indigenous ownership. This instability has scared off many investors who prefer smaller but surer returns elsewhere.

5. Institutional Framework

Often local laws don't adequately protect rights. Lack of an institutional framework can severely impact progress and investment.

6. The World Trade Organization

Many economists claim that the World Trade Organization (WTO) and other trading systems are biased against developing nations. Many developed nations adopt protectionist strategies which don't help liberalize trade.

I) CONSUMER PRICE INDEX:

The Consumer Price Index (CPI) is a measure that examines the weighted average of prices of a basket of consumer goods and services, such as transportation, food, and medical care. It is calculated by taking price changes for each item in the predetermined basket of goods and averaging them. Changes in the CPI are used to assess price changes associated with living costs; the CPI is one of the most frequently used statistics for identifying periods of inflation or deflation. CPI is widely used as an economic indicator. It is the most widely used measure of inflation and, by proxy, the effectiveness of the government's economic policy. The CPI gives the government, businesses, and citizens an idea about price changes in the economy and can act as a guide to make informed decisions about the economy.

J) CONSUMER PRICE INDEX AND US ECONOMY

The Consumer Price Index for All Urban Consumers (CPI-U) rose 0.3 percent in November on a seasonally adjusted basis. After rising 0.4 percent in October, the US Bureau of Labor Statistics reported today. Over the last 12 months, the all items index increased 2.1 percent before seasonal adjustment.

Increases in the shelter and energy indexes were significant factors in the seasonally adjusted monthly increase of the all-items index. Increases in the indexes for medical care, recreation, and food also contributed to the overall increase. The gasoline index rose 1.1 percent in November, and the other major energy component indexes also increased. The food index rose 0.1 percent, with the indexes for food at home and food away from home increasing over the month.

The index for all items less food and energy rose 0.2 percent in November, the same increase as in October. Along with the indexes for shelter, medical care, and recreation, the indexes for used cars and trucks and for apparel also rose in November. The new vehicles index fell in November, as did the index for airline fares.

The all-items index increased 2.1 percent for the 12 months ending November, a more significant rise than the 1.8- percent increase for the period ending October. The index for all items less food and energy rose 2.3 percent over the last 12 months. The food index rose 2.0 percent over the last 12 months, while the energy index declined 0.6 percent over the last year.

12-month percent change in CPI for All Urban Consumers (CPI-U), not seasonally adjusted, Nov. 2018 - Nov. 2019

Percent change
2.4
2.3
2.2
2.1
2.0
1.9
1.8
1.7
1.6
1.5

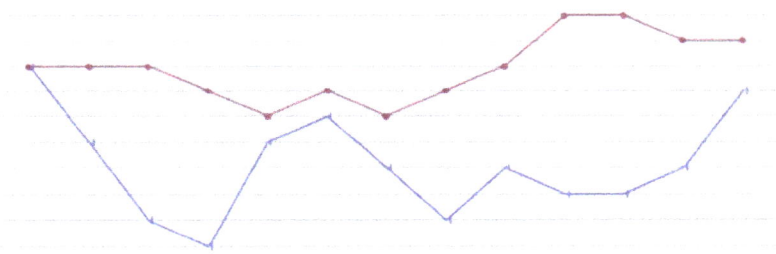

Nov'18 Dec Jan Feb Mar Apr May Jun Jul Aug Sep Oct Nov'19 All items
All items less food and energy

Table A. Percent changes in CPI for All Urban Consumers (CPI-U): US city average

	Seasonally adjusted changes from preceding month							Un- adjusted 12-mos. ended Nov. 2019
	May 2019	Jun. 2019	Jul. 2019	Aug. 2019	Sep. 2019	Oct. 2019	Nov. 2019	
All items	0.1	0.1	0.3	0.1	0.0	0.4	0.3	2.1
Food	0.3	0.0	0.0	0.0	0.1	0.2	0.1	2.0
Food at home	0.3	-0.2	-0.1	-0.2	0.0	0.3	0.1	1.0
Food away from home[1]	0.2	0.3	0.2	0.2	0.3	0.2	0.2	3.2
Energy	-0.6	-2.3	1.3	-1.9	-1.4	2.7	0.8	-0.6
Energy commodities	-0.4	-3.5	2.4	-3.3	-2.3	3.5	1.1	-1.5
Gasoline (all types)	-0.5	-3.6	2.5	-3.5	-2.4	3.7	1.1	-1.2
Fuel oil	-0.3	-2.3	0.6	-0.9	-0.8	0.8	1.4	-6.7

	Seasonally adjusted changes from preceding month							Un- adjusted 12-mos. ended Nov. 2019
	May 2019	Jun. 2019	Jul. 2019	Aug. 2019	Sep. 2019	Oct. 2019	Nov. 2019	
Energy services	-0.8	-0.7	0.0	-0.2	-0.1	1.8	0.4	0.6
Electricity	-0.8	-0.8	0.6	-0.3	0.0	1.6	0.3	0.5
Utility (piped) gas servics	-1.0	-0.3	-1.8	0.1	-0.7	2.4	1.1	1.1
All items less food and energy Commodities less food and energy	0.1	0.3	0.3	0.3	0.1	0.2	0.2	2.3
commodities	-0.1	0.4	0.2	0.2	-0.3	-0.1	0.0	0.1
New vehicles	0.1	0.1	-0.2	-0.1	-0.1	-0.2	-0.1	-0.1

Used cars and trucks	-1.4	1.6	0.9	1.1	-1.6	1.3	0.6	-0.4
Apparel	0.0	1.1	0.4	0.2	-0.4	-1.8	0.1	-1.6
Medical care commodities	-0.4	-0.2	0.2	0.3	-0.6	1.2	0.1	0.6
Services less energy services	0.2	0.3	0.3	0.3	0.3	0.2	0.3	3.0

Shelter	0.2	0.3	0.3	0.2	0.3	0.1	0.3	3.3
Transportation services	0.1	0.0	0.3	0.4	0.3	0.1	0.0	0.8
Medical care services	0.5	0.4	0.5	0.9	0.4	0.9	0.4	5.1

1 Not seasonally adjusted.

FOOD

The food index increased 0.1 percent in November, following a 0.2-percent rise the prior month. The index for food at home also rose 0.1 percent, after increasing 0.3 percent in October. Four of the six major grocery store food group indexes increased in November. The index for dairy and related products rose 0.6 percent over the month. The indexes for nonalcoholic beverages, meat, poultry, fish, eggs, cereals, and bakery products also increased in November.

The index for fruits and vegetables fell 0.7 percent in November after rising 0.9 percent in October, with the fresh fruit index declining 1.6 percent. The index for other food at home was unchanged over the month.

The indexes for full-service meals increased 0.3 percent in November, while the index for limited-service meals increased 0.1 percent over the month. The food away from home index has increased every month since being unchanged in June 2017. The food at home index increased 1.0 percent over the last 12 months. All the major grocery store food group indexes rose over the period, ranging from 0.4 percent (both the other food at home index and the fruits and vegetables index) to 2.6 percent (the dairy and related products index). The index for food away from home rose 3.2 percent over the last year, as the index for full-service meals increased 3.6 percent and the index for limited-service meals rose 3.0 percent.

ENERGY

The energy index increased 0.8 percent in November after rising 2.7 percent i n October. The gasoline index rose 1.1 percent in November, following a 3.7-percent increase in October. (Before seasonal adjustment, gasoline prices fell 1.1 percent in November.) Other major energy indexes also rose in November, with the index for natural gas rising 1.1 percent and the index for electricity increasing 0.3 percent.

The energy index declined 0.6 percent over the past 12 months. The gasoline index fell 1.2 percent, and the fuel oil index decreased 6.7 percent over the year. In contrast, the index for natural gas rose 1.l percent, and the index for electricity advanced 0.5 percent.

ALL ITEMS LESS FOOD AND ENERGY

The index for all items less food and energy increased 0.2 percent in November, as it did in October. The medical care index increased 0.3 percent. The index for hospital services also rose 0.3 percent, and the index for physicians' services increased 0.1 percent. The index for prescription drugs fell 0.1 percent in November after increasing 1.8 percent in October.

The shelter index rose 0.3 percent in November. The index for rent also rose 0.3 percent, while the index for owners' equivalent rent increased 0.2 percent over the month. The index for lodging away from home rose 1.1 percent in November after falling 3.8 percent in October. The education index and the apparel index both increased 0.1 percent over the month.

The recreation index rose 0.4 percent in November, after rising 0.7 percent in October. Most of its major component indexes increased, including cable a n d satellite television services (0.4 percent) and sporting goods (0.9 percent). The index for used cars and trucks rose 0.6 percent in November after rising 1.3 percent in October.

The new vehicles index fell 0.1 percent in November, its fifth consecutive decline the index for airline fares fell 0.9 percent in November, while the index for motor vehicle insurance fell 0.2 percent. The index for household furnishings and operations was unchanged in November.

The index for all items less food and energy rose 2.3 percent over the past 12 months. The shelter index rose 3.3 percent over the 12 months, and the medical care index rose 4.2 percent. Most other major component indexes increased over the 12 months, although the indexes for apparel, used cars and trucks, and motor vehicle insurance declined.

BRIEF EXPLANATION OF THE CPI:

The Consumer Price Index (CPI) measures consumers' prices for goods and services. The CPI reflects spending patterns for each population group: all urban consumers and urban wage earners, and clerical workers. The all-urban consumer group represents about 93 percent of the total US population. It is based on the expenditures of almost all residents of urban or metropolitan areas, including professionals, the self-employed, the poor, the unemployed, retired people, and urban wage earners and clerical workers. Not included in the CPI are the spending patterns of people living in rural nonmetropolitan areas, farming families, people in the Armed Forces, and those in institutions, such as prisons and mental hospitals. Two indexes measure consumer inflation for all urban consumers: the Consumer Price Index for All Urban Consumers (CPI-U) and the Chained Consumer Price Index for All Urban Consumers (C-CPI-U).

The Consumer Price Index for Urban Wage Earners and Clerical Workers (CPI-W) is based on the expenditures of households included in the CPIU definition that meet two requirements: more than one-half of the household's income must come from clerical or wage occupations, and at least one of the household's earners must have been employed for at least 37 weeks during the previous 12 months. The CPI-W population represents about 29 percent of the total US population and is a subset of the CPI-U population.

The CPIs are based on prices of food, clothing, shelter, fuels, transportation, doctors' and dentists' services, drugs, and other goods and services that people buy for day-to-day living. Prices are collected each month in 75 urban areas across the country from about 6,000 housing units and approximately 22,000 retail establishments (department stores, supermarkets, hospitals, filling stations, and other types of stores and service establishments). All taxes directly associated with the purchase and use of items are included in the index. Prices of fuels and a few other items are obtained every month in all 75 locations. Most other commodities and services are collected every month in the three largest geographic areas and every other month in other areas. Prices of most goods and services are obtained by personal visits, Emails, or telephone calls by the Bureau's trained representatives.

In calculating the index, price changes for the various items in each location are aggregated using weights, representing their importance in the spending of the appropriate population group. Local data are then combined to obtain a US city average. For the CPI-U and CPI-W, separate indexes are also published by size of the city, by region of the country, for cross- classifications of regions and population-size classes, and 23 selected local areas. Area indexes do not measure differences in prices among cities; they only measure the average change in prices for each area since the base period. For the C-CPI-U, data are issued only at the national level. The CPIU and CPI-W are considered final when released, but the C-CPI-U is issued in preliminary form and subject to three subsequent quarterly revisions.

The index measures price change from a designed reference date. For most of the CPI-U and the CPI-W, the reference base is 1982-84 equals 100. The reference base for the C-CPI-U is December 1999 equals 100.

An increase of 7 percent from the reference base, for example, is shown as 107.000. Alternatively, that relationship can also be expressed as the price of a base period market basket of goods and services rising from $100 to $107.

SAMPLING ERROR IN THE CPI

The CPI is a statistical estimate subject to sampling error because it is based upon a sample of retail prices and not the complete universe of all prices. BLS calculates and publishes estimates of the 1- month, 2-month, 6- month, and 12-month percent change standard errors annually for the CPIU. These standard error estimates can be used to construct confidence intervals for hypothesis testing.

APA – (ADVANCE PRICING AGREEMENT):

The US established the world's first formal APA program in 1991. The current program is called the Advance Pricing and Mutual Agreement (APMA) program. Unilateral, bilateral, and multilateral APAs are all available. Therefore, the APMA program may require special justification to enter into unilateral APA covering transactions involving a treaty partner for which a bilateral or multilateral APA would be available.

Taxpayers initiate the process for obtaining an APA by filing an APA request with the APMA program that meets the content requirements of Revenue Procedure 2015-41. The APA request generally must be filed by the date that the taxpayer files its income tax return for the first taxable year of the APA term. However, a taxpayer can obtain a 120-day extension to file an APA request by paying the applicable user fee (discussed below) by this date. Bilateral and multilateral APA requests must be filed within 60 days of the filing date of the APA request with the foreign tax competent authority. Among other substantive and procedural requirements, the APA request must include fully functional and factual analysis and proposals for one or more covered transactions, transfer pricing methods (and economic analysis to support such methods), critical assumptions, and an APA term. The user fee for an APA increased to US$113,500 effective January 1st 2019. Special reduced rates apply to renewal APAs and specific small business APAs.

The time required to obtain an APA can vary greatly depending on several factors, including the complexity of the transactions and the issues, the workload of the particular APMA staff members assigned to the case, and, in bilateral cases, the treaty relationship between the IRS and the particular foreign tax authority assigned. According to statistics released in the IRS's 2018 Announcement and Report Concerning Advance Pricing Agreements (APA Annual Report), the average completion time for APAs concluded in 2018 was 33.4 months for unilateral APAs and 45.6 months for bilateral APAs.

MLA- MILITARY LENDING ACT:

The Military Lending Act1 (MLA), enacted in 2006 and implemented by the Department of Defense (DoD), protects active-duty members of the military, their spouses, and their dependents from certain lending practices. These practices could pose risks for service members and their families and threaten military readiness and affect service member retention. The DoD regulation2 implementing the MLA contains limitations on and requirements for certain types of consumer credit extended to active duty service members and their spouses, children, and certain other dependents ("covered borrowers"). Subject to certain exceptions, the regulation generally applies to persons who meet the definition of a creditor in Regulation Z and are engaged in the business of extending such credit, as well as their assignees.3

For covered transactions, the MLA and the implementing regulation limit the amount a creditor may charge, including interest, fees, and charges imposed for credit insurance, debt cancellation and suspension, and other credit-related ancillary products sold in connection with the transaction.

As expressed through an annualized rate referred to as the Military Annual Percentage Rate (MAPR)4, the total charge may not exceed 36 percent.5 The MAPR includes charges that are not included in the finance charge, or the annual percentage rate (APR) disclosed under the Truth in Lending

Act(TILA).

In July 2015, DoD published revisions to the MLA implementing regulations that:

➣

- Extend the MLA's protections to a broader range of credit products;
- Modify the MAPR to include certain additional charges;
- Alter the provisions of the optional safe harbor available to creditors for identification of covered borrowers;
- Modify the disclosures creditors are required to provide to covered borrowers;
- Modify the prohibition on rolling over, renewing, or refinancing consumer credit; and
- Implement statutory changes, including provisions related to administrative enforcement and civil liability for MLA violations (for knowingly violating the MLA, there is potential for criminal penalties).

CHAPTER 6

G20 COUNTRIES

In September 1999, the finance ministers and central bank governors of the Group of Seven countries (the G-7) announced their intention to "broaden the dialogue on key economic and financial policy issues among systemically significant economies and promote co-operation to achieve stable and sustainable world economic growth that benefits all." This announcement marked the official birth of what subsequently became known as the Group of Twenty countries (the G-20).

This new international group was launched primarily to address challenges to international financial stability posed by the widening crisis in emerging economies that had begun in Asia in 1997.

Although ad hoc groups had been initially struck to deal with these issues, it became increasingly apparent that a permanent forum for informal dialogue between advanced and emerging economies was required.

The G-20, whose membership consists of systemically important advanced and emerging economies, representing all regions of the globe, the European Union, and the Bretton Woods institutions, filled an essential gap in the governance structure of the international economic and financial system.

The establishment of the G-20 recognized the considerable changes in the international economic landscape over the previous decades. The growing importance of emerging economies and the increasing integration of the global economy and financial markets underscored the importance of broadening international economic and financial cooperation.

The G-20's mandate was to help shape the international agenda, discuss economic and financial issues in areas where consensus had not yet been achieved, and "lead by example." In particular, the Group was seen as an essential forum for discussing ways to prevent and resolve international financial crises. A significant early achievement was its endorsement of internationally accepted standards and codes to improve economic and financial transparency and strengthen financial systems.

Following the 6 September 2001 terrorist attacks in the United States, member countries took a forceful stand against the financing of terrorism and encouraged all countries to follow suit. G-20 discussions also contributed to introducing collective action clauses in international bond contracts and adopting an informal code of conduct between primary sovereign borrowers and lenders. The Group has recently become an essential venue for discussing quota reform and representation at the International Monetary Fund.

Although its initial focus was on issues related to international financial stability, the G-20 has also examined a broad range of longer-term economic issues of interest to its membership. The G-20 played an important role in supporting globalization and ensuring that its benefits could be shared by all, including the least developing countries.

Other subjects studied included the effectiveness of aid programs, abuses of the financial system, development of domestic financial markets, regional economic integration, demographics, and resource security.

Since its inception, its membership and outside observers have come to view the G-20 as an important addition to the international architecture that has made a valued contribution to better global governance. The Group has been particularly successful in sharing experiences and exchanging views on key global issues, especially those that lend themselves to specific outcomes.

The keys to its success have been the ability of the Group to engage in meaningful debate, frankly and informally, and a commitment to seek consensus. The G-20 must continue to build on these successes since its future role will hinge on the ability of its members to continue to collaborate in a collegial and effective manner.

At a meeting of the Deputies of the Group of Twenty (G-20) countries held in Pretoria, South Africa on 24–25 March 2007, it was proposed that a Study Group be established to prepare a brief history of the G-20 since its inception in 1999. Deputies supported the proposal, and most G-20 members later took part in preparing this report.

First, with the Group's tenth-anniversary approach, it was an appropriate time to reflect on the forum's origins, development, and achievements. Second, it was deemed worthwhile to gather the views and perceptions of individuals who were key in establishing the Group before memories fade. While some remain in senior positions within their administrations, many have left the public service or have retired.

Third, an overview of the Group's activities and operations since its inception provides a helpful starting point from which to consider the effectiveness of the forum and its broader integration into the global economic and financial system.

In the preparation of this history, interviews were conducted with key officials involved in establishing this forum and took part in G-20 meetings during its formative years (Annex B). In addition, G-20 members provided their views on the objectives, work program, operational procedures, and the perceived effectiveness of the G-20. Past chairs also supplied summaries of their host years, along with supporting documents and communiqués (Annex C).

The Group of Twenty, or G20, is the premier forum for international cooperation on the most important international economic and financial agendas. It brings together the world's major advanced and emerging economies.

The G20 comprises Argentina, Australia, Brazil, Canada, China, EU, France, Germany, India, Indonesia, Italy, Japan,

Mexico, Russia, Saudi Arabia, South Africa, South Korea, Turkey, UK, and the USA. The G20 Countries together represent around 90% of global GDP, 80% of global trade, and two-thirds of the world's population.

The objectives of the G20 are a) Policy coordination between its members t o achieve global economic stability, sustainable growth; b) To promote financial regulations that reduce risks and prevent future financial crises, and c) To create a new international financial architecture.

ORIGIN AND EVOLUTION:

The G20 was created in response to both the financial crises that arose in several emerging economies in the 1990s and a growing recognition that some of these countries were not adequately represented in global economic discussion and governance. In December 1999, the Finance Ministers and Central Bank Governors of advanced and emerging countries of systemic importance met for the first time in Berlin, Germany, for an informal dialogue on key issues for global economic stability. Since then, Finance Ministers and Central Bank Governors have met annually. India hosted a meeting of G20 finance ministers and central bank governors in 2002. G20 was raised to the Summit level in 2008 to address the global financial and economic crisis of 2008. The G-20 operates without a permanent secretariat or staff.

The chair rotates annually among the members and is selected from a different regional grouping of countries. The chair is part of a revolving three-member management group of past, present, and future chairs referred to as the Troika. The current chair of the G-20 is Mexico; the next Chair will be Russia. The preparatory process for the G20 Summit is conducted through the established Sherpa and Finance tracks that prepare and follow up on the issues and commitments adopted at the Summits. The Sherpas' Track focuses on non-economic and financial issues, such as development, anti-corruption, and food security, while addressing internal aspects such as procedural rules of the G20 process. The Sherpas carry out important planning, negotiation, and implementation tasks continuously. The Finance Track focuses on economic and financial issues. The Sherpa and Finance tracks rely on the technical and substantive work of a series of expert working groups.

Additionally, the thematic plan is developed through several Ministerial Meetings, such as the Joint Meeting of Finance and Development Ministers and the Labor, Agriculture and Tourism Ministerial meetings. The G-20 in 2019 and 2020 Japan holds the rotating chair of the G-20 in 2019 and focused the summit agenda on three significant issues: trade, the digital economy, and the environment. As in recent summits, the US positions on trade and climate change put it at odds with the other G-20 members, with some analysts continuing to refer to the forum as the "G-19+1." In the communiqué, leaders agreed to general principles supporting trade (accessible, fair, non- discriminatory, transparent, predictable, and stable) and pledged to reform the World Trade Organization, but did not repeat previous pledges to fight protectionism. On climate change, the communiqué reflected the split between the United States, which has decided to withdraw from the Paris Agreement, and the other 19 countries, which pledged continued support for and implemented the Paris Agreement.

The communiqué also references commitments on a range of other issues, including infrastructure investment, global finance, anti-corruption, employment, women's empowerment, agriculture, development, global health, and migration, with varying consequence and degree of specificity. President Trump also held several high-profile meetings with leaders on the side of G-20 events, including with the crown prince of Saudi Arabia, Mohammed bin Salman, and Chinese President Xi Jinping. Saudi Arabia is to chair the G-20 in 2020 and host the summit on November 21-22, 2020, in Riyadh. Some analysts concerned about Saudi Arabia's human rights practices have called for relocation or boycott of the summit. However, it is not clear what traction such proposals have gained to date. US Leadership and Effectiveness of the G- 20 The G-20 meeting and outcomes contribute to the ongoing debate about the US leadership in the world under the Trump Administration.

Some commentators are concerned that US isolation at international summits reflects a growing trend of abdication of US leadership and abandonment of US allies. Others are more optimistic, arguing that differences between the United States and other countries are overblown and that President Trump is pursuing foreign policies consistent with his campaign pledges. Why is Russia not ranked among the G7 nations? The European Union has participated fully in the G7 since 1981 as a "none numerated" member. It is represented by the presidents of the European Council, which comprises the EU member states' leaders, and the European Commission, the EU's executive body. There are no formal criteria for membership, but the participants are all developed democracies.

The aggregate gross domestic product (GDP) of G7 member states makes up nearly 50 percent of the global economy in nominal terms, down nearly 70 percent three decades ago. The Group of Seven (G7) is an informal bloc of industrialized democracies— Canada, France, Germany, Italy, Japan, the United Kingdom, and the United States that meets annually to discuss global economic governance and international security issues, and energy policy. Proponents say the forum's small and relatively homogenous membership promotes collective decision-making, but critics note that it often lacks follow-through and excludes important emerging powers. Russia belonged to the forum from 1998 through 2014, when the bloc was known as the Group of Eight (G8) but was suspended following its annexation.

The G7's future has been challenged by continued tensions with Russia, disagreements over trade and climate policies, and the larger Group of Twenty's (G20) rise as an alternative forum. Meanwhile, US President Donald J. Trump has deepened divisions within the bloc, raising questions over cooperation on various policies. The forum originated with a 1975 summit hosted by France that brought together six governments: France, Germany, Italy, Japan, the United Kingdom, and the United States, thus leading to the name Group of Six or G6. The summit came to be known as the Group of Seven, or G7, in 1976 with the addition of Canada. With a substantial financial and economic weight, Russia was added to the political forum from 1997, which the following year became known as the G8.

In March 2014, Russia was suspended indefinitely following the annexation of Crimea; after that, the political forum name reverted to G7. In 2017 Russia announced its permanent withdrawal from the G8. However, several representatives of G7 countries stated that they would be interested in Russia's return to the group. The Group of Eight was an inter-governmental political forum from 1997 until 2014. It had formed from the Group of Seven after excluding the country of Russia and resumed operating under that name after Russia was disinvited in 2014. How the impact of the G7 nation on the USA? The first principle of the G7 trade acquis is the importance of free trade and investment for economic growth – which has set the tone for the trade section of nearly all G7/G8 leaders' communiqués of the past. As an example, at the 2016 Summit in Ise-Shima, the G7 Heads of State and Government declared that "trade and investment are key drivers of growth, the prosperity of our people and the achievement of sustainable development worldwide." 3 The second principle, which implicitly derives from the first, is the commitment to fight protectionism.

Such a principle has been included in virtually all G7/G8 leaders' communiqués since the Heads of State. France, (West) Germany, Italy, Japan, the UK, and the US met for the first time in Rambouillet in 1975 (Canada joined the fully-fledged G7 in 1976). Following Donald Trump's inauguration in January 2017, the United States began to question the G7 t rade acquis and its key principles, by introducing new, controversial concepts – such as "fair" and "reciprocal" trade – in the G7 process. Such concepts underpin the president's "America First" trade policy, whose declared goal is to eliminate the US bilateral trade deficits in goods. In the eyes of the Trump administration, these trade deficits would result from "unfair" trade deals signed by previous administrations and from "unfair" foreign trade practices, rather than from macroeconomic imbalances between domestic savings and investments, currency swings, or international capital flows.

The administration seems to be determined to pursue such a goal in various ways, which include:

- the renegotiation of existing trade agreements, such as the North Atlantic Free Trade Agreement (NAFTA) and the US-South Korea Free Trade Agreement (KORUS);
- the freezing of or withdrawal from negotiations over future trade agreements, such as the Transatlantic Trade and Investment Partnership (TTIP) with the EU and the Trans-Pacific Partnership (TPP) with eleven Asia-Pacific countries;
- the launch of negotiations on new trade and investment agreements at presumably more favorable conditions for the United States, but only in a bilateral fashion; and
- the adoption of unilateral trade remedies against countries allegedly responsible for trade wrongdoing. The developments that followed the G7 Summit in Taormina and the unilateral trade-restrictive measures adopted by the Trump administration reveal how difficult it will be to reaffirm the key principles of the G7 trade acquis at the 2018 Summit. After all, the Trump administration has now developed a more in-depth knowledge of the multilateral process. Fact sheets released by the White House following President Trump's State of the Union address on 30 January 2018 demonstrate this shift: "The President shaped Leaders Statements at the G7, G20, and APEC, ensuring that they highlighted concerns about unfair trade practices and promoted fair and reciprocal trade for the first time." Discussion of the BRICS (Brazil, Russia, India, China, and South Africa). Brazil, Russia, India, China, and South Africa (BRICS) are emerging protagonists in international development cooperation.

Over the last decade, BRICS have increased their financial and technical assistance and established distinct ways and means of economic cooperationwith developing countries. The progressive relevance of BRICS in economic respects is not yet reflected in political respects, which is why BRICS are seeking change in the architecture of international (development) politics. BRICS are at the forefront of using their economic weight to induce change, challenging traditional western donors in general and the EU in particular. Among the five countries, the role of South Africa is somewhat different as its economy is much smaller than that of the other four countries, and strictly speaking, the country does not comply with all the characteristics generally adopted to distinguish the country group:

1.)   The outstanding size of their economies,
2.)   Strong growth rates, leading to increasing significance in the world economy, and
3.)   The demand for a stronger political voice in international governance structures, which corresponds to their economic status. Nevertheless, BRICS are a heterogeneous group with individual countries also forming other coalitions. Besides the differentiation made above for South Africa, China is in an exceptional position at the other end concerning most aspects of economic cooperation, and Russia stands out as a former superpower.

Brazil, Russia, India, China, and South Africa (BRICS) are leading emerging economies and political powers at the regional and international levels. The acronym was originally coined in 2001 to highlight the exceptional role of critical emerging economies and only included Brazil, Russia, India, and China (BRIC). It was pointed out that high growth rates, economic potential, and demographic development were going to put BRIC further in a leadership position, and it was argued that their increased relevance should also be reflected in their incorporation to the G7 (O'Neill 2011) and their rivalry or importance to the USA.

One also has to keep in mind that BRICS are winners of the globalization process of the last decade (on average GDP) and are opting for participation a n d influence in rather than opposition to—multilateral economic and political institutions (G20, IMF, World Bank, World Trade Organization / WTO) (Skak 2011: 14/16).

There are mutual economic interests and interdependencies among BRICS, the US, and the EU. Thus, their political strategy is targeting multilateral negotiation and cooperation rather than confrontation and power politics. One of the exciting aspects of power distribution between the BRIC nations is the balance of power between these nations and the world and their policies.

When we examine this balance of power through two outlooks– Defensive Realism and Offensive Realism – we notice a common thread emerge. Of all the four BRIC nations, Brazil is the least influenced by a security dilemma, mostly given its location. It also has the added advantage of being the most powerful economy in South America, strengthening its position. That being said, Russia offers an entirely different perspective. As a former "threat" to the United States and a (declining) superpower with a significant weapons arsenal, Russia is more concerned about its role on the world stage.

Furthermore, the current Russian political climate does not lend itself well to a docile political outlook. But of all the four BRIC economies, perhaps the most striking security dilemma is between India and China, for obvious reasons. Geographically, China's proximity to one of America's strongest allies, Japan. Therefore, politically, as a secular English-speaking democracy, India and the United States have common ground that threatens the Chinese power base. However, with the increased interdependence on trade between all these nations and the United States, other factors take a backstage to trade. Therefore, given that the United States is not actively engaged in war (or at a political impasse) against any of these countries, it becomes easier to evaluate the security dilemma through an economic worldview. Henceforth, we will also add another economic bargaining tool to the mix: Public Debt.

The reason for this is that, unlike free trade, countries that hold American debt facilitate capital inflow and could therefore affect US interest rates. While reserve diversification by holders of

American debt is unlikely (given the lack of other suitable assets, except for gold), increased foreign debt and trade imbalances could yield a sovereign debt crisis for the United States. This is potential leverage for those countries that hold significant quantities of American debt. Before we get started, it is worthwhile to look at the External Debt vs. GDP for all the BRIC countries and the US and Japan. The reason for including Japan is that Japan is the largest holder of American debt and is an American ally outside of China. This, coupled with geographic proximity to China, could play a role in how China may perceive its leverage in holding American debt. These countries are break-away from the G20 nations, most notably China. International trade and investment declined sharply in the aftermath of the 2008 financial crisis. To coordinate policy responses in the wake of this crisis, the Group of Twenty (G20) was elevated to the leaders' level. The BRICS grouping of Brazil, Russia, India, China, and South Africa was founded as a summit to gather leaders from the most important emerging economies. This contribution reviews the work of both a to restore trade and investment.

Despite efforts to stimulate cross-border trade and investment, we show that neither has returned to pre-crisis levels. This is especially the case regarding international investment for the G20 members, although the data show a revival of trade. In general, BRICS members have been able to recover more quickly. Although members have not consistently implemented their decisions, the G20 and BRICS have proven effective for coordinating efforts, and compliance has been relatively high. Well, this contribution argues that more can be done, especially regarding investments. The future will tell whether these two bodies will continue to be complimentary and whether they will withstand protectionist and nationalist reflexes.

(https://limo.libis.be/primo-explore/fulldisplay?docid=LIRIAS1542390&context=L&vid=Lirias&search_scope=Lirias&tab=default_tab&lang=en_U omSitemap=1)

China and India are most commonly viewed in tandem as the two emerging powers with the potential to change the geopolitical order. Both exhibit deep frustrations over the way they have been treated within the global system. They come to the global governance table with a mutual sense of historical grievances and claims, albeit contested (Vieira and Alden 2011), to represent the interests of all developing countries. They share a neo- Westphalia commitment to state sovereignty and non-intervention. They proclaim the need for a rules-based, stable, and predictable world order that respects the diversity of political systems and stages of development.

China and India were expected to be agents of powerful change in multilateral fore to benefit the Global South. In contrast to the revisionist argument, the two emerging powers opted to attempt to reshape the contour of international politics by socializing "change" by engaging in and reinventing informal governance and institutions; the G20 and BRICS are two prime examples. Indeed, rebutting skepticism about the progress of BRICS, the two powers, despite mutual strategic rivalry on regional and global issues, successfully institutionalized cooperation in the form of the New Development Bank (NDB), and undertook coordinated initiatives on other non-traditional security areas. However, it is apparent that cooperation between China and India from within BRICS to beyond the BRICS framework, particularly in influencing the G20 agenda beyond international financial governance, is absent and mostly rhetorical and timid at best. To address the puzzle of why this is the case, this paper contends that the divergence in the two nations' leadership roles in seeking status attribution has weakened the prospect for broader and deeper cooperation between India and China in the G20 forum. Unlike China, India has not moved to host the G20 summit process at the leaders' level. Whereas the locus of China's defensiveness was focused on the United States and the rest of the West, India's defensiveness was in response to China. Having taken on the leadership role vis-à-vis the BRICS bank, India found itself at an explicit disadvantage in terms of diplomatic tools and at a material advantage as China took ownership of the initiative. To understand the dynamics of the roles of China and India in the G20 and BRICS, it is not enough to locate the two countries as twin "emerging" powers potentially challenging the United States.

There is also a need to locate them both in associative terms (in which they cooperate) and as competitors (in which they exist as strategic rivals).

Some similarity exists in the two countries' approach, above all in their defensive styles concerning the G20, but even these defensive styles display essential divergences. Though somewhat masked by an ordinary membership within the self-selective BRICS forum, the differences between China and India are evident on various issues, leading to a lack of meaningful cooperation in influencing the G20.

CHAPTER 7

INFLUENCE ON US ECONOMY

Have you ever said to yourself, "How exactly does the US economy work?" During a recession, you might think, "Not too well!" Learn the causes of recession by understanding gross domestic product and the laws of supply and demand. Know how the federal government uses fiscal and trade policy GDP: Everything the US economy produces is measured by GDP. When the GDP growth rate turns negative, the economy enters a recession. Supply and Demand: Supply and demand are the forces that drive the US economy. Supply includes labor, represented by employment, and natural resources, such as oil, land, and water. Demand, or personal consumption, drives almost 70% of the economy

INFLATION AND DEFLATION:

Inflation occurs when demand is more significant than supply and prices go up . Your income and the rate at which it keeps up with rising prices determine how much inflation impacts your life. The opposite is deflation; it occurs when prices fall. That also happens to assets, such as housing prices and stock portfolios. That creates stock crashes and economic crises. Deflation is worse than inflation for an economy. Fiscal Policy: Fiscal policy is the $4 trillion federal budget. The federal budget is the government's estimate of revenue and spending for each fiscal year. Like a family budget, the federal budget itemizes the expenditure of public funds for the upcoming fiscal year. The federal government's fiscal year begins each October first.

All the revenue ultimately comes from taxes on your income, so you need to know how it is spent. Fiscal policy can stimulate, guide, or depress the economy, but only business can create economic growth.

The difference between a budget deficit, a trade deficit, and the national debt are as below:

a) The national debt is the total amount of government borrowing still outstanding owed to individuals and institutions.

b) The budget deficit is the amount by which government spending exceeds government revenues

c) The trade deficit is when the value of a nation's imports exceeds the value of its exports. Monetary Policy: The primary objective of monetary policy is to control inflation. Its secondary objective is to stimulate the economy. It is also charged with the smooth functioning of the banking system.

Trade Policy: Trade policy affects the cost of imports and exports by regulating trade agreements with other countries. Like the North American Free Trade Agreement, trade agreements seek to reduce trade costs and increase each country's GDP. Financial Markets: The building blocks are stocks and stock investing. They are riskier than bonds. The safest are Treasury bonds. The riskiest are junk bonds. You can invest in either with mutual funds.

A) ECONOMIC DEVELOPMENT IN U.S:

Why are people in the United States, Germany, and Japan so much richer today than 100 or 1000 years ago? Why are people in France and the Netherlands today so much richer than people in Haiti and Kenya? Questions like these are at the heart of the study of economic growth. Economics seeks to answer these questions by building quantitative models that can be compared with empirical data. That is, we'd like our models to tell us not only that one country will be more prosperous than another, but by how much. Or to explain not only that we should be richer today than a century ago, but that the growth rate should be 2% per year rather than 10%.

Growth economics has only partially achieved these goals. It may be a critical input into our analysis, knowing where the goalposts lie, knowing the facts of economic growth. Growth in economic activity brings about benefits to economic actors, and it is the predominant measure of changes in material living standards. In general, as GDP grows, individuals' incomes increase, as does the production of goods and services. So, as economic activity increases, individuals not only have access to more goods and services, but they also have more income to purchase those goods and services. Therefore, GDP growth does not give any indication of how income growth is distributed within the economy. Some factors fuel economic growth, and which factors are most important differ depending on the timescale with which policymakers are concerned... In the near term, growth in economic activity is primarily governed by the business cycle, which shifts from expansionary phases to contractionary phases (recessions), and recoveries. Policymakers can use monetary and fiscal policies to affect aggregate demand (i.e., total spending) to diminish the volatility of changes in economic growth due to the business cycle.

However, these policies are unlikely to have a significant impact on the economy's long-term growth rate. The long-term growth rate is primarily determined by the amount of physical capital, human capital, and technological change in the economy. Seven years after the financial crisis, the United States is making a comeback. While modest by historical standards, the US economic recovery has been one of the strongest in the OECD, thanks to robust monetary policy support and an early fiscal expansion. Many private-sector jobs have been created, pushing unemployment down to its pre-crisis level, thereby providing consumers with higher income and improving their confidence.

Further economic growth at a pace near 2% a year is likely in the short term, while a new recession is a low-probability prospect in the current environment. But several long-term challenges remain unresolved. In particular, the slowdown of productivity growth already apparent since the mid-2000s has continued in recent years. Faster productivity growth – supported by well-designed investments in innovation, infrastructure, skills, and inclusiveness – would help address future challenges such as rising income inequality, population aging, and fiscal sustainability.

Against this background, this report focuses on:

- How to support a sustainable expansion by using fiscal and structural policies to lighten the burden on monetary policy and to facilitate normalization of interest rates;
- How to boost productivity growth by bolstering competitive forces on market incumbents, combined with well-designed investments in innovation, skills, infrastructure, and environmental protection
- How to make growth more inclusive by enabling the acquisition of appropriate skills, eliminating obstacles to employment, and enabling individuals to fulfill their potential after the recovery, growth is likely to remain moderate Output has recovered, albeit more slowly than in previous expansions The slow speed of the recovery reflects the severity and depth of the financial crisis, fiscal consolidation, the exit of baby boomers from the labor market, weaknesses in crucial OECD economies, and, more recently, world trade stagnation induced by the slowdown of China and lower demand from oil-exporting countries. While activity is, on average, well above pre-crisis peaks, the revival does not prevail everywhere.

The recovery has been particularly robust in some locations, but activity remains low in other areas. Some industries have performed strongly (software, telecommunications, pharmaceutical products), while growth in many other areas and industries remains mired in the doldrums. The diversity in economic outcomes is reflected in income inequality, which continues to increase. The recovery has been sustained mainly by mutually reinforcing gains in employment, income, and household spending. Declines in energy prices – that began when oil and natural gas became available from unconventional sources – have boosted household purchasing power, providing an additional lift to consumption. Therefore, the impetus from these influences is unlikely to be sustained without a meaningful pickup in real wage growth. Business capital expenditure, which is needed to increase productivity, has been low even as corporate profitability is at multi-decade highs.

Instead of investing, companies have opted to return earnings to shareholders through dividends and share buybacks, accounting for a larger share of profits than in the past.

B) ALLIES WITH OTHER ECONOMY COOPERATION:

The US-China economic relationship has reached a critical juncture. Over the past year, the US has imposed tariffs on $250 billion worth of Chinese imports, and China has retaliated, raising tariffs on US exports. At the G-20 leaders' summit in November 2018, Presidents Trump and Xi agreed to resolve the trade dispute within 90 days— by March 1, 2019, though this deadline has been recently extended. The US concerns that underpin these bilateral trade tensions stem from specific practices endemic to China's economic model that systematically tilt the playing field in favor of Chinese companies domestically and globally. Progress on specific trade issues will require China to comply with its World Trade Organization (WTO) commitments and make specific reforms that will likely touch on areas of state control over the economy. In addition, new trade rules are needed to address China's economic practices not covered by its WTO commitments, including in areas such as state-owned enterprises (SOEs), certain subsidies, and digital trade. These issues also come at a time of increasing US concern over China's national security risks, particularly concerning technology access.

Despite the challenges the US has had at the WTO, the WTO should be central to resolving US-China trade tensions. From this perspective, we outline a multipronged strategy, including bilateral, multilateral, and unilateral actions and working with allies that together would constitute positive next steps for this critical economic relationship. In taking this multifaceted approach, the US also needs to stay true to its values and not accept short-term gains or "fig leaf" deals. In particular, creating a managed trade relationship with China would not be a constructive outcome. The resulting deal should address the real issues at hand in a free Joshua P. Meltzer and Neena Shenai POLICY BRIEF February 2019 the US-China economic relationship A comprehensive approach 2 The US-China economic relationship: A comprehensive approach market manner and strengthen the multilateral global trading system and the rule of law that the US has championed in the post-World War II era. All of these matters underscore the complexity of US-China bilateral negotiations as well as the stakes at play.

Resolving US-China differences in a meaningful way will take time. A key part of the US strategy concerning the China challenge needs to include new trade agreements with allies, which raise the standards for trade. This strategy would benefit the parties to such free trade agreements (FTAs) and create economic costs to China from nonparticipation, which should further encourage China to reform its economy and trade practices to join the new trade agreements.

The Trans-Pacific Partnership (TPP), from which the US withdrew in 2017, included important new rules in areas that matter for the US, such as on SOEs, IP, digital trade, transparency, and due process in the making of regulations affecting trade. With China outside the trading block, TPP would have created costs for China. According to one estimate, TPP could have decreased Chinese income by $40 billion annually, and this would have grown as more countries joined the agreement.10 Taken together, TPP would have been an important part of the "comprehensive toolkit" USTR refers to in creating pressure on China to reform. The TPP has now been reconstituted without the US as the Comprehensive and Progressive

TPP (CPTPP) and most of the rules for addressing US concerns with Chinese trade practices remain. The importance of the CPTPP for addressing the China challenge warrants the US to reconsider its position on the agreement and rejoin. If bilateral FTAs remain the focus, for the time being, the US should aim to conclude agreements with its strategic allies in the Asia-Pacific region and beyond.

C) FINANCIAL STABILITY:

A stable financial system, when hit by adverse events or "shocks," continues to meet the demands of households and businesses for financial services, such as credit providers and payment services. In contrast, in an unstable system, these same shocks are likely to have much larger effects, disrupting the flow of credit and lending to declines in employment and economic activity.

Consistent with this view of financial stability, the Federal Reserve Board's monitoring framework distinguishes between shocks to and vulnerabilities of the financial system. Shocks, such as sudden changes to financial or economic conditions, are typically unpredictable and inherently difficult to predict. Vulnerabilities tend to build up over time and are the aspects of the financial system most expected to cause widespread problems in times of stress. As a result, the framework focuses primarily on monitoring vulnerabilities and emphasizes four broad categories based on research. Elevated valuation pressures are signaled by asset prices that are high relative to economic fundamentals or historical norms and are often driven by an increased willingness of investors to take on risk. As such, elevated valuation pressures imply a greater possibility of outsized drops in asset prices. Excessive borrowing by businesses and households leaves them vulnerable to distress if their incomes decline or the assets they own fall in value. In the event of such shocks, businesses and households with high debt burdens may need to cut back spending sharply, affecting the overall level of economic activity.

Moreover, when businesses and households cannot make payments on their loans, financial institutions and investors incur losses. Excessive leverage within the financial sector increases the risk that financial institutions will not have the ability to absorb even modest losses when hit by adverse shocks. In those situations, institutions will be forced to cut back lending, sell their assets, or, in extreme cases, shut down.

Such responses can lead to credit crunches in which access to credit for households and businesses is substantially impaired. Funding risks expose the financial system to the possibility that investors will "run" by withdrawing their funds from are hard to sell quickly or in assets with a long maturity. This liquidity and maturity transformation can create an incentive for investors to withdraw funds quickly in adverse situations. Facing a run, financial institutions may need to sell assets quickly at "fire sale" prices, thereby incurring substantial losses and potentially even becoming insolvent. Historians and economists often refer to widespread investor run as "financial panics." These vulnerabilities often interact with each other. For example, elevated valuation pressures tend to be associated with excessive borrowing by businesses and households. Both borrowers and lenders are more willing t o accept higher degrees of risk and leverage when asset prices are appreciating rapidly. The associated debt and leverage, in turn, make the risk of outsized declines in asset prices more likely and more damaging. Similarly, the risk of a run on a financial institution and the consequent fire sales of assets are greatly amplified when significant leverage is involved.

It is important to note that liquidity and maturity transformation and lending to households, businesses, and financial firms are key aspects of how the financial system supports the economy. For example, banks provide safe, liquid assets to depositors and long-term loans to households and businesses; businesses rely on loans or bonds to fund investment projects, and households benefit from a well-functioning mortgage market when buying a home. The Federal Reserve's monitoring framework also tracks domestic and international developments to identify near-term risks, plausible adverse developments, or shocks that could stress the US Financial system. The analysis of these risks focuses on assessing how such potential shocks may play out through the US financial system, given our current assessment of the four areas of vulnerabilities. While this framework provides a systematic way to assess financial stability, some potential risks do not fit neatly into it because they are novel or challenging to quantify. For example, cybersecurity and developments in crypto-assets are the subjects of monitoring and policy efforts that may be addressed in future discussions of risks. In addition, some vulnerabilities are difficult to measure with currently available data, and the set of vulnerabilities may evolve. Given these limitations, we continually rely o r. ongoing research by the Federal Reserve staff, academics, and other experts to improve our measurement of existing vulnerabilities and to keep pace with changes in the financial system that could create new forms of vulnerabilities or add to existing one's particular institution or sector. Many financial institutions raise funds from the public with a commitment to return their investors' money on short notice. Still, those institutions then invest much of the funds in illiquid assets (non-monetary) that are hard to sell quickly or in assets with a long maturity.

This liquidity and maturity transformation can create an incentive for investors to withdraw funds quickly in adverse situations. Facing a run, financial institutions may need to sell assets quickly at "fire sale" prices, thereby incurring substantial losses and potentially even becoming insolvent. Historians and economists often refer to widespread investor run as "financial panics." These vulnerabilities often interact with each other. For example, elevated valuation pressures tend to be associated with excessive borrowing by businesses and households. Both borrowers and lenders are more willing t o accept higher degrees of risk and leverage when asset prices are appreciating rapidly.

The associated debt and leverage, in turn, make the risk of outsized declines in asset prices more likely and more damaging. Similarly, the risk of a run on a financial institution and the consequent fire sales of assets are greatly amplified when significant leverage is involved. It is important to note t h a t liquidity and maturity transformation and lending to households, businesses, and financial firms are key aspects of how the financial system supports the economy. For example, banks provide safe, liquid assets to depositors and long-term loans to households and businesses; businesses rely on loans or bonds to fund investment projects, and households benefit from a well-functioning mortgage market when buying a home. The Federal Reserve's monitoring framework also tracks domestic and international developments to identify near-term risks—that is, plausible adverse developments or shocks that could stress the US. Financial system. The analysis of these risks focuses on assessing how such potential shocks may play out through the US financial system, given our current assessment of the four areas of vulnerabilities. While this framework provides a systematic way to assess financial stability, some potential risks do not fit neatly into it because they are novel or challenging to quantify. For example, cybersecurity and developments in crypto-assets are the subjects of monitoring and policy efforts that may be addressed in future discussions of risks.3 In addition, some vulnerabilities are difficult to measure with currently available data, and the set of vulnerabilities may evolve.

Given these limitations, we continually rely on ongoing research by the Federal Reserve staff, academics, and other experts to improve our measurement of existing vulnerabilities and keep pace with changes in the financial system that could create new vulnerabilities or add to existing ones. Our view on the current level of vulnerabilities is as follows:

1.) Asset valuations. Valuation pressures remain elevated in a number of markets, with investors continuing to exhibit a high appetite for risk, although some pressures have eased a bit since the November 2018 FSR.

2.) Borrowing by businesses and households. Borrowing by businesses is historically high relative to gross domestic product (GDP), with the most rapid increases in debt concentrated among the riskiest firms amid signs o f deteriorating credit standards. In contrast, household borrowing remains at a modest level relative to incomes,

Surviving in a Buoyant Economy | 107

and the debt owed by borrowers with credit scores below prime has remained flat.

3.) Leverage in the financial sector. The largest US banks remain strongly capitalized, and the leverage of broker-dealers is substantially below pre- crisis levels. Insurance companies appear to be in relatively strong financial positions. Hedge fund leverage appears to have declined over the past six months.

4.) Funding risk. Funding risks in the financial system are low Estimates of the total outstanding amount of financial system liabilities that are most vulnerable to runs, including those issued by nonbanks, remain modest relative to levels leading up to the financial crisis. Short-term wholesale funding continues to be low compared with other liabilities, and the ratio of high-quality liquid assets to total assets remains high at large banks.

D) WOMEN EMPOWERMENT:

Empowerment is a multidimensional process that should enable individuals or a group of individuals to realize their whole identity and powers in all spheres of life. According to Webster's dictionary, the word empowerment indicates the situation of authority or to be authorized or to be powerful. Empowerment is a process that gives a person freedom in decision-making.

What is women's empowerment? Women empowerment means the emancipation of women from the vicious grips of social, economic, political, caste, and gender-based discrimination. It means granting women the freedom to make life choices. Women Empowerment itself elaborates that Social Rights, Political Rights, Economic stability, judicial strength, and all other rights should also be equal to women. There should be no discrimination between men and women. (https://www.iaspaper.net/women- empowerment-in-india)

Empowerment is an aid to help women achieve equality with men or reduce the gender gap considerably. Gender equality and female empowerment are now universally recognized as core development objectives, fundamental for realizing human rights, and key to effective and sustainable development outcomes. No society can develop sustainably without increasing and transforming the distribution of opportunities, resources, and choices for males and females so that they have equal power to shape their own lives and contribute to their communities. A growing body of research demonstrates that societies with greater gender equality experience faster economic growth and benefit from greater agricultural productivity and improved food security. Empowering women to participate in and lead public and private institutions makes these institutions more representative and effective. Increasing girls' and women's education and access to resources improve the health and education of the next generation. Women also play critical roles as effective peace advocates, community leaders, and civil and human rights champions.

Gender equality concerns women and men. It involves working with men and boys, women and girls to bring about changes in attitudes, behaviors, roles, and responsibilities at home, in the workplace, and the community. Genuine equality means more than parity in numbers or laws on the books; it means expanding freedoms and improving the overall quality of life. Equality is achieved without sacrificing gains for males or females. Female empowerment is achieved when women and girls acquire the power to act freely, exercise their rights, and fulfill their potential as full and equal members of society. While empowerment often comes from within, and individuals empower themselves, cultures, societies, and institutions create conditions that facilitate or undermine the possibilities for empowerment. Gender integration involves identifying and addressing gender inequalities during strategy and project design, implementation, and monitoring and evaluation. Since the roles and power relations between men and women affect how an activity is implemented, project managers must address these issues regularly. A large body of evidence has established that gender inequality has costs for individuals and societies, and these costs can multiply across generations. For instance, women's economic dependency on men reduces their ability to exercise safer sex options to protect themselves against unwanted pregnancies and HIV infection.

When women cannot participate in the labor force, are prevented by law or practice from entering certain occupations, or are excluded from management positions, GDP growth can suffer by as much as two percent. Conversely, gender equality not only benefits individual males and females but whole sectors and societies. For instance, the Food and Agriculture Organization of the United Nations (FAO) estimates that if women had the same access to productive resources as men, they could increase yields on their farms by 20 to 30 percent, which in turn could raise total agricultural output in developingcountries by 2.5 to 4 percent and reduce the number of hungry people in the world by 12 to 17 percent, up to 150 million people. Great strides have been made to reduce gender gaps and improve the status of women and girls over the past three decades. Yet, significant gender gaps remain across sectors in all countries worldwide; they are often greater among the poor. Historically, gender inequalities have disadvantaged females, and while that remains the case in many domains, gender norms and policies also negatively affect boys and men in specific regions and sectors.

E) BUSINESS ENVIRONMENT:

As stated earlier, the success of every business depends on adapting itself to the environment within which it functions. For example, when there is a change in the government policies, the business has to make the necessary changes to adapt itself to the new policies. Similarly, a technology change may render the existing products obsolete. We have seen that computer technology has replaced typewriters; the color television has made the black and white television out of fashion.

Again, a change in the fashion or customers' taste may shift the demand in the market for a particular product, e.g., the demand for jeans reduced the sale of other traditional wear. All these aspects are external factors that are beyond the control of the business. So, the business units must adapt themselves to these changes to survive and succeed in business. Hence, it is necessary to have a clear understanding of the concept of business environment and its various components. The term 'business environment' connotes external forces, factors, and institutions beyond the control of the business and affects the functioning of a business enterprise. These include customers, competitors, suppliers, government, social, political, legal, technological, etc. While some of these factors or forces may directly influence the business firm, others may operate indirectly.

Thus, the business environment may be defined as the total surroundings, which directly or indirectly bear on the functioning of the business. It may also be defined as the set of external factors, such as economic factors, social factors, political and legal factors, demographic factors, technical factors, etc., which are uncontrollable and affect a firm's business decisions.

FEATURES OF BUSINESS ENVIRONMENT:

Based on the above discussion, the features of the business environment can be summarized as follows.

a.) The business environment is the total of all external factors to the business firm that greatly influence its functioning.

b.) It covers factors and forces like customers, competitors, suppliers, government, and the social, cultural, political, technological, and legal conditions.

c.) The business environment is dynamic, which means it keeps on changing.

d.) The changes in the business environment are unpredictable. It is complicated to predict the exact nature of future happenings and economic and social environment changes.

e.) Business Environment differs from place to place, region to region, and country to country. Political conditions in the United States differ from those in Iran. Taste and values cherished by people in India and China vary considerably.

IMPORTANCE OF BUSINESS ENVIRONMENT:

There is a close and continuous interaction between the business and its environment. This interaction helps in strengthening the business firm and using its resources more effectively. As stated above, the business environment is multifaceted, complex, and dynamic and has a far-reaching impact on the survival and growth of the business. To be more specific, a p r o p e r understanding of the social, political, legal, and economic environment helps the business in the following ways:

a) Determining Opportunities and Threats: The interaction between the business and its environment would identify opportunities for and threats to the business. It helps the business enterprises to meet the challenges successfully.

b) Giving Direction for Growth: The interaction with the environment leads to opening up new frontiers of growth for the business firms. It enables the business to identify the areas for growth and expansion of their activities.

c) Continuous Learning: Environmental analysis makes the task of managers easier in dealing with business challenges. The managers are motivated to continuously update their knowledge, understanding, and skills to meet the predicted changes in the business realm.

d) Image Building: Environmental understanding helps business organizations improve their image by showing their sensitivity to the environment within which they are working. For example, many companies have set up Captive Power Plants (CPP) in their factories to meet their own requirement of power given the shortage of power.

e) Meeting Competition: It helps firms analyze the competitors' strategies and formulate their own strategies accordingly.

f) Identifying Firm's Strength and Weakness: The business environment helps identify the individual strengths and weaknesses of technological and global developments.

Confining business environment to uncontrollable external factors may be classified as

a)   Economic environment; and

b)   Non-economic environment. The economic environment includes economic conditions, economic policies, and the economic system of the country. Non-economic environment comprises social, political, legal, technological, demographic and natural environment. All these have a bearing on the strategies adopted by the firms and any change in these areas is likely to have a far-reaching impact on their operations.

CHAPTER 8

INFLUENCES OF PUBLIC AND PRIVATE SECTOR ON US ECONOMY

The economic activities of the public sector-Federal, state, and local government are extensive. We begin by discussing the economic functions of governments. What is the government's role in the economy? Providing the Legal Structure Government provides the legal framework and the services needed for a market economy to operate effectively. The legal framework sets the legal status of business enterprises, ensures private ownership rights, and allows the making and enforcement of contracts. The government also establishes the legal "rules of the game" that control relationships among businesses, resource suppliers, and consumers. Discrete units of government referee economic relationships, seek out foul play and impose penalties.

Government intervention is presumed to improve the allocation of resources. By supplying a medium of exchange, ensuring product quality, defining ownership rights, and enforcing contracts, the government increases the volume and safety of exchange. This widens the market and fosters greater specialization in the use of land, labor, capital, and entrepreneurial resources. Such specialization promotes a more efficient allocation of resources. Like the optimal amount of any "good," the optimal amount of regulation is that the marginal benefit and marginal cost are equal. Thus, either too little regulation (MB exceeds MC) or too much regulation (MB is more minor than MC). The task is to decide wisely on the right amount. Maintaining Competition is the primary regulatory mechanism in the market system. It is the force that subjects producers and resource suppliers to the dictates of consumer sovereignty. With competition, buyers are the boss, the marker is their agent, and businesses are their servants. It is a different story where a single seller-a monopoly-controls an industry. By controlling supply, a monopolist can charge a higher-than-competitive price. Producer sovereignty then supplants consumer sovereignty. In the United States, the government has attempted to control monopoly through regulation and through antitrust. A few industries are natural monopolies-industries in which technology is such that only a single seller can achieve the lowest possible costs. In some cases, the government has allowed these monopolies to exist and created public commissions to regulate their prices and set their service standards. Examples of regulated monopolies are some firms that provide local electricity, telephone, and transportation services.

However, in nearly all markets, efficient production can best be attained with a high degree of competition. Therefore, the Federal government has enacted a series of antitrust (antimonopoly) laws, beginning with the Sherman Act of 1890, to prohibit certain monopoly abuses and, if necessary, break monopolists up 'into competing firms. Under these laws, for example, in 2000, Microsoft was found guilty of monopolizing the market for operating systems for personal computers. Rather than breaking up Microsoft, well, the government imposed a series of prohibitions and requirements that collectively limited Microsoft's ability to engage in anticompetitive actions.

REDISTRIBUTING INCOME:

The market system is impersonal and may distribute income more inequitably than society desires. It yields substantial incomes to those whose labor, under inherent ability and acquired education and skills, commands high wages. Similarly, through hard work or inheritance, those who possess valuable capital and land receive large property incomes. But many other members of society have the less productive ability, have received only modest amounts of education and training, and have accumulated or inherited no property resources. Moreover, some of the elderly, the physically and mentally disabled, and the poorly educated earn small incomes or, like the unemployed, no income at all. Thus, society chooses to redistribute a part of total income through various government policies and programs. Transfer payments, such as welfare checks and food stamps, provide relief to the needy, the dependent, the disabled, and older citizens; unemployment compensation payments provide aid to the unemployed. Market intention Government also alters the distribution of income through market intervention, that is, by acting to modify the prices that are or would be established by market forces. Providing farmers with above-market prices for their output and requiring that firms pay minimum wages are illustrations of government interventions designed to raise the income of specific groups. The government uses the personal income tax to take a more significant proportion of the rich's income than the poor, thus narrowing the attar-tax income difference between high-income and low-income earners.

The extent to which government should redistribute income is subject to lively debate. Redistribution involves both benefits and costs. The purported benefits arc greater "fairness" or "economic justice"; the purported costs are reduced incentives to work, save, invest, and produce, and therefore a loss of total output and income. Correcting for Positive Externalities How might government deal with the under-allocation of resources resulting from positive externalities? The answer is either to subsidize consumers (to increase demand), to subsidize producers (to increase suppler, or, in the extreme, to have government produce the product: To correct the under allocation of resources to higher education, the US government provides low- interest loans to students so that they can afford more education. Those loans increase the demand for higher education. Subsidize suppliers in some cases, government finds it more convenient and administratively simpler to correct an under allocation by subsidizing suppliers. For example, in higher education, state governments provide substantial portions of the budgets of public colleges and universities.

Such subsidies lower the costs of producing higher education and increase i t s supply. Publicly subsidized immunization programs, hospitals, and medical research are other examples. A third policy option may be appropriate where positive externalities are extremely large: Government may finance or, in the extreme, own and operate the industry that is involved. Examples are the US Postal Service and Federal air traffic control systems. Public Goods and Services Certain goods called private goods are produced through the competitive market system. Examples are the wide variety of items sold in stores. Private goods have two characteristics—Rivalry and excludability. "Rivalry" means that when one person buys and consumes a product, it is not available for purchase and consumption by another person. What Joan gets, Jane cannot have. Excludability means that buyers who are willing and able to pay the market price for the product obtain its benefits, but those unable or unwilling to pay that price do not. This characteristic enables profitable production by a private firm. Certain other goods and services called public goods to have the opposite characteristics of non- rivalry and non-excludability.

Everyone can simultaneously obtain the benefit from a public good such as a global positioning system, national defense, street lighting, and environmental protection. One person's benefit does not reduce the benefit available to others. More important, there is no practical way of excluding individuals from the benefit of the good once it comes into existence. The inability to exclude creates a free-rider problem, in which people can receive benefits from a public good without having to pay for it. As a result, goods and services subject to free-riding will typically be unprofitable for any private firm that decides to produce and sell them. An example of a public good is the war on terrorism. This public good is thought to be economically justified by most Americans because the benefits are perceived as exceeding the costs. However, once the war efforts are undertaken, the benefits accrue to all Americans (no rivalry). And there is no practical way to exclude any American from receiving those benefits (no excludability). No private firm will undertake the war on terrorism because the benefits cannot be profitably sold (due to the free-rider problem). So here, we have a service that yields substantial benefits but to which the market system will not allocate sufficient resources. Like national defense in several, the pursuit of the war on terrorism is public food. Society signals its desire for such goods by voting turn particular political candidates who support their provision. Because of the free-rider problem, the public sector provides these goods and finances them through compulsory charges in the form of taxes.

CHAPTER 9

ECONOMIC FACTS AND EFFECTS
THAT IMPACT US ECONOMY

The sizeable economic size of the United States and its close linkages with t h e world economy would suggest that US growth could significantly influence growth in other countries. In 2000, US GDP was equivalent to over one-fifth of world GDP on a purchasing power parity basis and nearly a third of nominal world GDP at market exchange rates.3 The United States accounted for over one-fifth of the expansion in real-world GDP during the past two decades and nearly a quarter of the expansion during 1992-2000. World and US growth have moved closer together in recent decades, with a correlation coefficient of over 80 percent. US growth on growth in other countries depends in part on the significance of the United States in other countries' external trade. Table 1 compares the importance of the five major trading partners in the world economy, the United States, France, Germany, Japan, and the United Kingdom—in the external trade of a sample of 147 countries. The United States has the highest average weight as well as the highest average ranking. On average, it is among the four most important trading partners for other countries, and it is the most important trading partner for forty-nine countries.

(Notable) The Agreement between the United States of America, the United Mexican States, and Canada (USMCA) is a <u>free trade agreement</u> between <u>Canada</u>, <u>Mexico</u>, and the <u>United States</u>. It replaced the <u>North American Free Trade Agreement</u> (NAFTA) implemented in 1994 and is sometimes characterized as "NAFTA 2.0".

On July 1, 2020, the new trade agreement between the United States, Mexico, and Canada began. Each participating country has its name for it and collectively may be referred to as USMCA or USMCA/T-MEC/CUSMA.

- In the United States, it is the **United States-Mexico-Canada Agreement** (USMCA).
- In Mexico, it is the **Tratado entre México, Estados Unidos y Canadá** (T-MEC).
- In Canada, it is the **Canada-United States-Mexico Agreement** (CUSMA).

The text of the Agreement is posted on the U.S. Trade Representative's website at the following URL: https://ustr.gov/trade-agreements/free-trade-agreements/united-states-mexico-canada-

For additional information, see - http://ustr.gov/usmca.

- The overall economic effects of the North American Free Trade Agreement (NAFTA) on the economies of the United States, Mexico, and Canada.
- The critical NAFTA provisions and related legal changes for the United States, Mexico, and Canada that may significantly affect individual sectors; and
- NAFTA's short and long-term impact on important industrial, energy, agricultural, and service sectors of the US economy remained long-term. The key NAFTA provisions affecting US-Mexican investment and trade include removing tariffs and quotas, the imposition of

strict and transparent rules of origin, and the limitation on duty drawback. NAFTA also will require changes in Mexican law or the maintenance of recent Mexican reforms to ensure removal of many restrictions on FDI, more robust intellectual property protection, and a more open services market and government procurement process for US firms. * NAFTA prohibits adopting new customs duties on qualifying goods and contains a schedule of staged duty reductions for each party, divided into four general staging categories plus a category for goods remaining free of duty. The staged duty reductions affecting US trade with Mexico are approximate (based on a percentage distribution of 1990 trade).

Under NAFTA, the United States and Canada will gain greater access to the Mexican market, which currently is the fastest-growing major export market f o r US goods and services. Second. NAFTA will create investment opportunities that will facilitate trade among the member countries in many sectors, reducing impediments to future trade growth. Third. NAFTA will lead to a more predictable business environment, reducing risks associated with investment and other business decisions. Fourth, NAFTA will improve the competitive position of specific US sectors in North American and global markets. Finally, NAFTA is an essential step towards free trade throughout the hemisphere. However, as noted below, NAFTA is also likely to affect specific US sectors adversely. Trade and investment within North America are essential to all these nations. The United States and Canada's major trading partner and Mexico are the United States' third-largest partners after Canada and Japan. In 1991, Canada accounted for 19 percent of US merchandise trade, Japan 15 percent, and Mexico 7 percent. The United States is Mexico's largest trading partner and source of foreign direct investment (FDI), accounting for almost 70 percent of total Mexican trade in 1991 and 61 percent of Mexico's cumulative FDI by value as of June 1992. Mexico is likely to benefit substantially more from NAFTA than either the United States or Canada because its gross domestic product (GDP) is only 5 percent of US GDP.

Historically, its economy has been closed, and trade with the United States i s relatively more important to its economy. The United States-Mexico- Canada Agreement (USMCA)! The United States-Mexico-Canada agreement was made to replace the existing treaty that was formed to control the trade that was taking place in North America nation (Outside of the USA) . The deal was meant to take the position of NAFTA, the trade negation that was made by the heads of states of the United States, Mexico, and Canada. However, the agreement was subject to ratification by some parties within the government (Gantz, 2019). The agreement was believed to impact the targeted countries' economic situation with both losers and winners. What is the Agreement? The agreement was created to open a favorable forum where different parts of it can be negotiated and appropriate decisions made to improve economic development. The agreement was signed to re-energize the North American Free Trade Agreement (NAFTA), which was discussed and approved in the year 1994 (Hufbauer, & Globerman, 2018). Through the use of the USMCA, it was believed that economic growth would be generated coupled with improved living standards of all the targeted three countries. What the Agreement Offers? The agreement purposively offers the guideline for governing different types of trade and investment within the member countries. The deal, therefore, acted as the concrete foundation for promoting the prosperity of the Canadian State. It will, therefore, ensure that Canada serves as a valuable example of the country which enjoyed the benefits of trade liberalization compared to other countries across the globe since the agreement provided the mechanisms for governing the trade investments (Hufbauer, & Globerman, 2018).

Ideally, the deal offers a friendly atmosphere that will later contribute towards reinforcing of stable and sustainable economic relationship of Canada with the United States and Mexico. The Winners of the Agreement The first winner of the agreement was the American CEOs; the heads of different businesses in America got the certainty on trade. The deal was not significant as the one for China. Still, traders no longer had the possibility that President Trump could order the United States to pull out of NAFTA, which could plunge different states into chaos (Gantz, 2018). USMCA was therefore expected to improve the economy of the United States. The other winner in the agreement was the Lighthizer, the US trade, which Robert E. was managing. It won due to the more prominent US free trade deal, which was the finishing line since 1994 (Gantz, 2018). This was not considered an easy task hence celebrated as the victory. The other winner of the agreement was Canada. They managed to provide much of the economic development tools to Trump. The Canadian opened up the dairy market and were able to comply with and kept the chapter 19 dispute settlement process that assisted in dodging the US courts.

The losers of the Agreement Mexico is one of the losers of the agreement. The country allowed three countries to take part in most of the negotiations. The country needed Trump off their back as their economic development state was not going on well as expected. The USMCA managed to close up most of the factories in Mexico, where the labor cost was affordable to the employers (Gantz, 2018). The other loser was China since they could not make the trading deal with Trump.

A) CLIMATE EFFECTS ON US ECONOMY:

This study aims to advance understanding of the potential consequences of global climate change by examining the overall effect on the US economy of predicted impacts in key market activities that are likely to be particularly sensitive to future climate trends. These activities include crop agriculture a n d forestry, energy services related to heating and cooling, commercial water supply, and the protection of property and assets in coastal regions. Also considered are the effects on livestock and commercial fisheries and the increased storm, flood, and hurricane activity costs. Finally, the analysis accounts for population-based changes in labor supply and consumer demand due to climate-induced mortality and morbidity.

In each of these areas, impacts were modeled to estimate their aggregate effect on national measures of economic performance and welfare, including gross domestic product (GDP), consumption, investment, labor supply, capital stock, and leisure. At present, our knowledge of the direct or indirect impacts of climate change on a broad range of economic activities is incomplete. Accordingly, important sectors and activities such as tourism are omitted from this effort. Similarly, there is little information concerning possible interactions among the benefits and costs in different sectors. For example, the impacts on crop and livestock agriculture may have consequences for human health. Given the absence of reliable insights into such externalities or spillovers, these effects are also excluded from consideration. These limitations suggest that the results of this analysis are likely to understate the potential market impacts of climate change. More importantly, this analysis does not consider the non-market impacts of climate change, such as changes in species distributions, reductions in biodiversity, or losses of ecosystem goods and services. These considerations are essential to a complete evaluation of the consequences of climate change but are very difficult to value in economic terms. A companion Pew Center report, A Synthesis of Potential Impacts of Climate Change on the United States, provides more detail on the relative vulnerability of different US regions to both the market and non-market impacts of climate change.

To capture the range of market consequences potentially associated with climate change in the United States and to address the considerable uncertainties that exist, several distinct scenarios were developed for this analysis. Each incorporates different assumptions about the magnitude of climate change over the next century and about the direction and extent of likely impacts in the market sectors analyzed. Specifically, three different levels of climate change (low, central, and high) were considered in combination with two sets of market outcomes (optimistic and pessimistic) for a total of six primary scenarios. In terms of climate, the low, central, and high scenarios encompass projected increases in average temperature ranging from 1.

7oC to 5.3oC (3.1- 9.5oF) by 2100, together with precipitation increases ranging from 2.1 to 6.6 percent and sea-level rise ranging from 17.2 to 98.9 cm (7-40 inches) same period. In terms of impacts, the optimistic and pessimistic scenarios reflect a spectrum of outcomes from the available literature concerning the sensitivity of each sector to climatic shifts and its ability to adapt. As one would expect, the optimistic scenarios generally project either more minor damages or more significant benefits for a given amount of climate change than pessimistic scenarios. Because several of the market sectors included here are especially sensitive to changes in precipitation, two additional scenarios were analyzed. The first assumes the high degree of temperature change combined with lower precipitation ("high and drier"). In comparison, the second assumes the low level of temperature change combined with higher precipitation ("low and wetter"). By introducing the sector-specific damages (or benefits) associated with each of these scenarios into a computable general equilibrium model that simulates the complex interactions of the US economy as a whole, the combined effect of climate impacts across multiple sectors could be assessed in an integrated fashion.

Detailed results are described in the body of this report, but five principal conclusions emerge:

1.) Based on the market sectors and range of impacts considered for this analysis, projected climate change has the potential to impose considerable costs or produce temporary benefits for the US economy over the twenty-first century, depending on the extent to which pessimistic or optimistic outcomes prevail.

2.) Due to threshold effects in specific key sectors, the economic benefits simulated for the twenty-first century under optimistic assumptions are not sustainable and economic damages are inevitable.

3.) The effects of climate change on US agriculture dominate the other market impacts considered in this analysis.

4.) For the economy, wetter is better. All else being equal, more precipitation is better for agriculture —and hence better for the economy—than less precipitation. Not surprisingly, reductions in precipitation are costlier at higher temperatures than at lower temperatures and the negative impacts of drier climate conditions are greater under pessimistic assumptions than they are under optimistic assumptions.

5.) Changes in human mortality and morbidity are small but important determinants of the modeled impacts of climate change for the US economy as a whole. An increase in climate-induced mortality or illness reduces the population of workers and consumers available to participate in the market economy, leading to a loss of real GDP.

IMPACT OF CHINESE ECONOMY ON US ECONOMY:

With high growth rates during the past two decades and the largest trade surplus with the United States, China is the primary target of the US trade war efforts. Tariffs are the first shot in bilateral tensions that are multilateral zing and injuring global economic integration, coupled with ever more intense technology competition. The evolving global scenarios of US-China trade and technology conflicts are the outcome of an ever more anxious America forsaking its multilateral cooperative stances for primacy doctrines. In the worst case, these conflicts may escalate into a "decoupling" of both economies and cause a lasting global recession and new geopolitical confrontation. This gloomy scenario has become viable with the exceptional use of executive power by the post-9/11 US administrations. The Trump administration, in particular, is predicated on the "imperial presidency" that relies on an emergency status quo, new campaign finance, and "big money," which poses significant risks not only to US-China relations but also to American democracy and existing international order.

The United States and China are the world's leading powers in terms of the size of their economies, defense budgets, and global greenhouse gas emissions. Both nations are permanent members of the United Nations Security Council. In 2017, they were each other's largest trading partners. This bilateral relationship is perceived by many to be the most consequential in the world. The global importance of the US and Chinese economies, as measured by their nominal gross domestic product (GDP), can be illustrated in two ways that will also illuminate the challenges of the ongoing power transition: one involves the rise of the Chinese economy relative to the US GDP; the other focuses on the accompanying shifts in globalization. In 2000, China's economy was barely a tenth of the US GDP.

But after China became a member of the World Trade Organization (WTO) in 2001, its export-led growth soared in the 2000s, when its share of the US economy more than tripled from 12 percent in 2000 to over 40 percent in 2010. The original Goldman Sachs estimate was that China would surpass the United States in the late 2020s. The US-China economic relationship has reached a critical juncture. Over the past year, the US has imposed tariffs on $250 billion worth of Chinese imports, and China has retaliated, raising tariffs on US exports. At the G-20 leaders' summit in November 2018, Presidents Trump and Xi agreed to resolve the trade dispute within 90 days by March 1, 2019, though this deadline has been recently extended. The US concerns that underpin these bilateral trade tensions stem from specific practices endemic to China's economic model that systematically tilt the playing field in favor of Chinese companies domestically and globally. Progress on specific trade issues will require China to comply with its World Trade Organization (WTO) commitments and make certain reforms that will likely touch on areas of state control over the economy.

In addition, new trade rules are needed to address China's economic practices not covered by its WTO commitments, including in areas such as state-owned enterprises (SOEs), certain subsidies, and digital trade. These issues also come at a time of increasing US concern over China's national security risks, particularly concerning technology access. Despite the challenges the US has had at the WTO, the WTO should be central to resolving US-China trade tensions. From this perspective, we outline a multipronged strategy, including bilateral, multilateral, and unilateral actions and working with allies that together would constitute positive next steps for this critical economic relationship.

In taking this multifaceted approach, the US also needs to stay true to its values and not accept short-term gains or "fig leaf" deals. In particular, creating a managed trade relationship with China would not be a constructive outcome. The resulting deal should address the real issues at hand in a free. To assess what might constitute a sustainable economic relationship in the future, it is essential to be clear about the costs and benefits of US trade and investment with China. The US-China economic relationship delivers more benefits to the US than is commonly understood. For example, recent data shows that US exports to China support around 1.8 million jobs in services, agriculture, and capital goods.1 However, trade with China has also led to job destruction in some US industries, particularly low-wage manufacturing. Despite these costs, the frequent focus by the administration on the bilateral deficit is not a meaningful yardstick for assessing US-China trade or its impact on employment. The US trade deficit is less a product of restrictions on US imports than it reflects a low US domestic savings rate, which requires overseas capital to fund US domestic investment needs and the growth in US government debt. In addition, the trade deficit does not account for the activities of affiliates of US and Chinese companies in each respective market, a calculus that shows the US selling more to China than vice versa China's economic model has a range of growing implications for the US and globally. First, the move towards self-sufficiency in emerging technologies is inconsistent with a trading system based on comparative advantage.

Second, the use of SOEs, their access to subsidies, and the limited rule of l a w in China support state companies within China and globally. Third, China's industrial policy to pick winners is expected to lead to excess production and dumping overseas. This has already occurred, for instance, in steel and solar photovoltaic (PV) with negative impacts for US and global industries,2,3 and is expected to occur in more advanced industries identified in China's recent industrial policies, such as robotics, high-speed rail production, new energy vehicles, and batteries. Making progress in US-China economic relations in seeking mutually beneficial outcomes, the US should take a comprehensive approach to the negotiations based on market- orientated solutions, strengthening the global trading system and the rule of law. Bilateral negotiations US-China bilateral outcomes need to be verifiable, enforceable, and market-based— not simply a restatement of prior Chinese commitments such as to do better on IP protection and enforcement or forced technology transfer, or to buy more US products.

The bilateral track should include commitments from China to implement all of its WTO commitments. Additional WTO-plus commitments should be negotiated in SOEs, cross-border data flows, and determining the application of nonmarket economy (NME) status for trade remedy purposes. Where feasible, enforcement should be through the WTO dispute settlement mechanism, and recourse to arbitration under Article 25 of the Dispute Settlement Understanding (DSU) could be used to produce speedier results.

CHAPTER 10

A MANAGEMENT STRUCTURE THAT DEPICTS A TYPICAL (OFF- SHORE) MNC (MULTINATIONAL CORPORATION)

Globalization is the single most significant development changing business dynamics in this century. The reality of global markets and global competition is pervasive. The forces driving the world toward greater globalization are more significant than the forces that restrain this move. With the improvements in transportation and communication technologies, there is a sea change in how the companies are run. International trade leads to international marketing, which in turn leads to growth in international business. The phenomenal growth in international business brought about some new concepts in international management. The old theories of international trade focused upon natural resources and crude measures of factor endowments. Newer models focus upon the actual sources of competitive advantage of companies in industries. Ultimately, competitive advantage is based upon understanding what customers need and want and how to deliver these needs and wants with a competitive advantage. The formula that guides this task is V=B/P: value = benefits divided by price.

The greater the benefits and the lower the price, the greater the value. The task of the global company is to deliver value to customers located in Surviving global markets. The ability of corporations of all sizes to use globally available factors of production is an important factor in international competitiveness. A single Barbie doll is made in more than ten countries- designed in the United States, with parts and clothing from Japan, Korea, Italy, and Taiwan, assembled in Mexico and sold in different countries.

EVOLUTION OF MULTINATIONAL CORPORATION:

The dynamics of international business created a great need for the evolution o f Multinational corporations. A multinational corporation is a company engaged in producing and selling goods or services in more than one country. It usually consists of a parent company located in the home country and a few or more foreign subsidiaries. Some MNCs have more than 100 foreign subsidiaries scattered around the world. The globally coordinated resource allocation by single centralized management differentiates the multinational enterprise from other firms engaged in international business. MNCs make decisions about market-entry strategy; ownership of foreign operations; and production, marketing, and financial activities with an eye to what is best for the corporation as a whole. The proper multinational corporation emphasizes group performance rather than the performance of its parts. There are different types of multinational companies, such as;

a) Raw-Material Seekers: Raw-material seekers were the earliest multinationals and they aimed to exploit the raw materials that could be found overseas. The modern-day counterparts of these firms, the multinational oil and mining companies such as British Petroleum, Exxon Mobil, International Nickel, etc.,

b) **Market Seekers:** The market seeker is the archetype of the modern multinational firm that goes overseas to produce and sell in foreign markets. Examples include IBM, Toyota, Unilever, Coca-Cola.

c) Cost Minimizers: Cost minimizers are a relatively recent category of firms doing business internationally. These firms seek out and invest in lower-cost production sites overseas (for example, Hong Kong, Malaysia, Taiwan, and India) to remain cost-competitive both at home and abroad. MNCs have to follow the changes in macroeconomic factors, environmental and social issues, and business and industry developments. These factors will all profoundly shape the corporate landscape in the coming years. The following section deals with these trends. 1) Trends affecting the Corporate World: Those who say that business success is all about execution are wrong. The right product markets, technology, and geography are critical components of long-term economic performance.

Destructive industries usually trump good management; however: in sectors such as banking, telecommunications, and technology, almost two- thirds of the organic growth of listed Western companies can be attributed to being in the right markets and geographies. Companies that ride the currents succeed; those that swim against them usually struggle. Predicting short-term changes or shocks is often a fool's errand. But forecasting long-term directional change is possible by identifying trends by analyzing deep history rather than the shallow past. Even the Internet took more than 30 years to become an overnight phenomenon.

Let us take note of the ten trends that will change the business landscape. We have divided them under three broad categories:

a.) Macroeconomic trends;
    1.) New Centers of Economic Activity:
    2.) Role of the Public sector:
    3.) Changing global marketplace:
b.) Social and environmental trends;
    1.) Communication Technology:

      2.)   The battlefield for talent will shift.

      3.)   Corporate Accountability,

      4.)   Natural Resources:

c.) Business and industry trends;

      1.)   New global industry structures are emerging,

      2.)   Management will go from art to science,

      3.)   Ubiquitous access to information is changing the economics of knowledge. Studies of corporate expansion overseas indicate that firms become multinational by degree, with foreign direct investment being a late step in a process that begins with exports.

A) MULTINATIONAL COMPANIES AND US ECONOMY:

The contribution to the American economy of US multinational companies is increasingly being called into question.* Critics contend that these companies have "abandoned" the United States and that policy needs to rebalance their domestic and international operations. This report demonstrates that US multinational companies are, first and foremost, American companies. They perform large shares of America's productivity-enhancing activities capital investment, research and development, and trade, leading to jobs and high compensation. The central role of US multinational companies in underpinning US economic growth and job creation is even more critical today as the United States seeks to address the challenges presented by the current economic environment. Strong US multinational companies that can compete effectively in foreign markets will be better positioned to help America out of recession. The ability of US multinational companies to stem job losses in the United States and eventually return to hiring more American workers depends on the health, vitality, and competitiveness of their worldwide operations.

    The worldwide operations of US multinationals are highly concentrated in America in their US parents, not abroad in their foreign affiliates. The idea that US multinationals have somehow "abandoned" the facts do not support the United States. They maintain a significant presence in America, both relative to the overall US economy and relative to the size of their foreign affiliates. ➤ International engagement drives the overall strength of US multinational companies. Although the United States is still the world's largest single-country market, it has been a slow-growth market in the past generation compared with much of the world. Even with today's worldwide recession, this means that the overall strength of US multinationals is increasingly tied to their success in both America and abroad.

It also means that viewing the domestic and foreign operations of US multinationals as unrelated is increasingly incorrect. US multinationals must make strategic investment and employment decisions from a truly global perspective, with links across all locations and with dynamic variation in successful strategies both across companies at a point in time and within companies over time.

Foreign-affiliate activity tends to complement, not substitute for, key parent activities in the United States such as employment, worker compensation, and capital investment. Being globally engaged requires US multinationals to establish operations abroad and expand and integrate these foreign activities with their US parents. The idea that global expansion tends to "hollow out" US operations is incorrect. Instead, the scale and scope of US parent activities increasingly depend on successful engagement abroad.

Expansion by US parents and their affiliates contributes to the productivity a n d average standard of living of all Americans. US parent companies perform large shares of America's productivity-enhancing activities that lead to the high average compensation for American workers

- Output: Parent companies accounted for 24.9% of all private-sector output (measured in terms of gross domestic product) over $2.5 trillion.
- Capital Investment: Parent companies purchased $442.6 billion in new property, plant, and equipment, 31.3% of all private-sector capital investment.

- Exports: Parent companies exported $495.1 billion of goods to the rest of the world. This constituted nearly half 48.0% of the US total.

- Research and Development: To discover new products and processes, parent companies performed $187.8 billion of research and development. This was 75.8% of the total R&D performed by all US companies. All these productivity-enhancing activities contribute to larger average paychecks for the millions of employees of US multinationals.

- Parent companies employed over 21.7 million US workers. This was 19.1% of total private-sector payroll employment.

- Total compensation at US parent companies was over $1.36 trillion, a per- worker average of $62,784. This average was $12,163, fully 24.0% above the average for the rest of the private sector of $50,621. US parents purchased a total of $5.76 trillion in intermediate inputs. Of this total, 89.1% $5.14 trillion was bought from other companies in the United States. The worldwide operations of US multinational companies are highly concentrated in America in their US parents, not abroad in their foreign affiliates.

- Employment: Parent companies account for 69.6% of worldwide employment of US multinationals 21.7 million parent workers versus 9.5 million at affiliates. This translates into a ratio of almost 2.3 US employees for every affiliate employee.

- Output: Parent companies account for 71.6% of worldwide output (in terms of value-added) of US multinationals over $2.5 trillion versus about $1.0 trillion.

- Capital Investment: Parent companies undertake 74.3% of worldwide capital investment by US multinationals—$442.6 billion versus just $153.2 billion. For every $1 in affiliate capital expenditures, parents invested $2.89 worth in the United States.

- Research and Development: Parent companies perform 86.8% of worldwide R&D by US multinationals: $187.8 billion versus just $28.5 billion, or $6.59 in parent knowledge discovery for every $1 by affiliates. Foreign affiliates are located primarily in high-income countries that in many ways have economic structures similar to the United States, not in low-income countries.

- Affiliates in high-income countries accounted for 79% of total affiliate output and 90% of the output by all affiliates newly established or acquired. One of the main drivers of the global engagement of US multinationals is accessing foreign customers. New customers abroad can expand a company's revenues and profitability much more than the US market alone. The numbers here are striking. Today the United States remains the world's largest single-country market, with a 2008 GDP of $14.3 trillion. Serving this immense market remains a powerful imperative for US multinationals as the statistics of the previous chapter underscored. Despite the still-large size of the US economy, the United States has been a slow growth market in the past generation compared with much of the world. From 1990 through 2008, growth in US gross domestic product averaged 2.7%. Although respectable relative to earlier US periods, this was slow compared to what much of the world achieved during this time:

- 1990-2007 averages of 3.4% for the overall world, 4.6% for emerging and developing countries as a whole, 6.3% for India, and a remarkable 9.9% for China. These growth-rate differentials carry significant implications for the evolving size of national markets and, thus, prospective customers. At an annual growth rate of 2.8%, the US market doubles in size every twenty-five years. The comparable doubling periods for India and China are just 11.4 and 7.3 years, respectively. And despite the recession in many parts of the world today, these growth-rate differentials are widely forecast to persist into the future. If the past becomes a prologue, it takes the US market to double its current size. The Chinese market will expand more than tenfold. The bottom line here is that US multinationals must expand their access to foreign customers to achieve substantial revenue growth.

How exactly do US companies access customers abroad? Exporting is often the first (and often only) mode that comes to mind. But is exporting the full story? Not for multinational companies, which also access foreign customers via host-country affiliate sales. Indeed, accessing foreign customers via affiliate sales rather than exporting is a business imperative for many US multinationals. In many services lines of business, US multinationals simply must establish on-the-ground foreign affiliates if they want to access foreign customers. And these service-oriented businesses constitute the majority of US multinational activity. In 2006, non- manufacturing parents accounted for 58.3% of total parent value-added output ($1.46 trillion of $2.51 trillion); that same year, non-manufacturing affiliates similarly accounted for 54.2% of total affiliate value-added output ($540.1 billion of $995.6 billion).

Beyond US multinationals producing goods and services, there are also those involved in resource exploration and extraction, such as petroleum, natural gas, other commodities, and agriculture. For these companies, not only are their customers often spread around the globe but so, too, are the primary materials they need to access and add value to. Expansion abroad for these firms is essential for all parts of their business. The key point of the above discussion is that US multinationals must make strategic investment and employment decisions from a truly global perspective.

Moreover, globally competitive business models are not "one size fits all," neither at a point in time across companies nor even over time within each company itself. Each company has a uniquely rich history that informs its current structure and strategies. As such, each multinational needs the freedom to respond differently to globalization's evolving opportunities and pressures. Indeed, this dynamic process of discovery where and 138 | how to hire, invest, research, and sell is critical for US multinationals achieving and sustaining global competitiveness.

CHAPTER 11

INTELLECTUAL PROPERTY AND US ECONOMY

The Office of International Intellectual Property Enforcement (IPE) represents the genius of America to the world. Reflecting America's imagination, intellectual property is the lifeblood of our economy. The Office of Intellectual Property Enforcement (IPE) advocates for the adequate protection and enforcement of intellectual property rights (IPR) worldwide. The IPE team works closely with US ambassadors and diplomats serving worldwide to ensure that the interests of American rights holders are represented overseas and to highlight the integral role that IPR protection plays in supporting global innovation and economic growth.

IPE promotes robust intellectual property rights systems:

- to deter access to counterfeit and pirated goods that can harm consumers;
- to ensure that the interests of American IP rights holders are protected abroad;
- to promote IP protection and enforcement as vital for economic development. Surviving in a Buoyant Economy What are intellectual property rights? Intellectual property

(IP) refers to a brand, invention, design, or other kinds of creation, which a person or business has legal rights over.

Almost all businesses own some form of IP, which could be a business asset. Common types of IP include Copyright which protects written or published works such as books, songs, films, web content and artistic works. Patents this protects commercial inventions, e.g., a new business product or process. Design right this protects designs, such as drawings or computer models. Trademarks this protects signs, symbols, logos, words or sounds that distinguish your products and services from those of your competitors. IP can be either registered or unregistered. With unregistered IP, you automatically have legal rights over your creation.

Unregistered forms of IP include copyright, unregistered design rights, common law trademarks, and database rights protection for confidential information and trade secrets. With registered IP, you will have to apply to an authority, such as the Intellectual Property Office in the UN, to have your rights recognized. If you do not do this, others are free to exploit your creations. Registered forms of IP include patents, registered trademarks, and registered design rights. Treaties and reciprocal agreements: The USA is a signatory to the following international IP agreements: the Paris Convention under this, any person from a signatory state can apply for a patent or trade mark in any other signatory state, and will be given the same enforcement rights, and status as a national of that country would be y the Berne Convention under this, each member state recognizes the copyright of authors from other member states in the same way as the copyright of its own nationals by the Madrid Protocol this is a central system for obtaining a "bundle" of national trademark registrations in different jurisdictions, through a single application the Patent Co-operation Treaty this works in much the same way as the Madrid Protocol, but for patent applications. The USA is not a signatory to the Hague Agreement, which allows the protection of designs i n multiple countries through a single filing. Intellectual property rights - systems in the USA Copyright:

In the United States, creative work is automatically protected by copyright as long as it is both original, i.e., independently created and not copied from someone else's work. Fixed in a tangible form, i.e., easy to see, reproduce, or communicate over a long period. Copyright only protects the tangible form of your creative work. It does not protect the idea itself, only the form it takes. For example, suppose your business has an advertisement. In that case, the actual content is protected by copyright, but it does not prevent others from using a similar idea to create their own advertisement.

Although registration of copyright is not a legal requirement in the USA, it is advisable. This is because it establishes a public record of ownership and strengthens your position in the case of copyright infringement is necessary to press charges for copyright infringement in Federal courts is necessary to prevent infringing imports from entering the USA and allows you to claim statutory damages and attorney's fees in the case of copyright infringement rather than needing to prove actual damages.

As the copyright owner, only you have the right to copy, change, distribute or publicly display the work, or authorize others to do so. However, employ other companies or freelancers for specific works. It could be that they own the copyright, e.g., an external graphics designer may own the copyright for their commissioned work. It is therefore recommended that you always use a contract to clarify who owns the IP. The USA is a signatory to the Berne Convention on copyright. Under this, each member state recognizes the copyright of authors from other member ber states in the same way as the copyright of its own nationals Intellectual Property Rights in the USA. In the USA, work created on or after 1 January 1978 is protected for the life of the author plus seventy years if the owner is a person ninety-five years from publication or 120 years from the creation of the work, whichever is shorter if the owner is a corporation or other entity All other work created before 1978 is governed by the Copyright Act of 1909.

This provides initial protection of 28 years, with the chance of subsequent renewal. If the copyright of published material has expired, it is usually considered in the public domain, making it accessible for anyone to use. Patents: A patent is a governmental grant that allows someone to protect an invention. In the USA, the United States Patent and Trademark Office (USPTO) issues three kinds of patents: Utility patents for technological advances and innovations. This lasts a minimum of 20 years from the date of application. Design patent for new and original designs for items. This lasts for a fourteen-year term. Plant patent for the invention or discovery of any distinct and new plant varieties that have been asexually reproduced by grafting or selective cuttings (without seed manipulation). This protection is different to plant variety protection which the United States Department of Agriculture administers.

This lasts for a twenty-year term from the date of application. If you need to pitch an invention or design that has not yet been patented, you should use a non-disclosure agreement or obtain a provisional patent application. You should also keep any documents relating to the invention or design. The September 2011 America Invents Act (AIA) amended US patent law to make it a "first inventor to file" system, which is in line with other patent systems, including the UK. The "first inventor to file" system means that whoever files a patent application first can be awarded a patent. The AIA first-inventor-to- file provisions became effective on March 16 2013. US law also allows a one-year grace period for an investor to register a patent from the date of public disclosure. You should note that this is different from European countries, where public disclosure could prevent you from obtaining a patent.

Trademarks: Unlike copyright, trademarks are not automatic and are generally only protected if registered in the USA. Trademark rights are established through registration in most countries. This is known as "First to File." However, in the USA, as in the UK, the ownership of a trademark is established by whoever first uses it in commerce. This is known as the 'First to Use' system and requires you to use the mark connected with goods or services to protect your trademark. Therefore, if there is a dispute between you and another party over a trademark, whoever used it first commercially will own the right, even if they did not register it. However, to completely protect your trademark in the USA, you should also register it through the USPTO.

Registering your trademark also provides several further benefits to you, including y publicly declaring your ownership of the trademark y helping you to register your trademark in other countries y helping you to bring any legal action to the Federal courts, and preventing infringing material from being imported by allowing you to use the registered trademark symbol with your trademark. Because registration is not a requirement, there is no limit to the duration of a trademark in the USA. As long as there is the continued use of the trademark, ownership of the trademark right is maintained.

Registering and enforcing your intellectual property rights in the USA: Some types of intellectual property (IP) rights in the USA are automatic, but it is recommended that you always register them to both protect yourself and to make the most of your IP rights. "Priority rights" under the Paris Convention can help in the local registration of trademarks, designs, and patents by allowing rights previously registered elsewhere to become effective in the USA if filed within a time limit. As a signatory of the Paris Convention, the USA must also protect unfair competition in line with the rules of the Convention. Enforcing your IP rights in the USA: It is your responsibility to protect your IP, though governmental authorities can help you take steps to prevent and stop any infringements.

You should actively monitor the marketplace for any unauthorized use of your IP. If you think that a person or business has unlawfully used your IP, you should take expert legal advice before contacting an offender or pursuing any sort of litigation. IP law in the USA is complex and should only be used when other enforcement methods have failed to prevent an infringement. If litigation is necessary, then you should use a lawyer who specializes in IP law. Litigation takes place before either civil courts or administrative tribunals. It is also possible to take action against foreign offenders through the Federal court or by initiating investigations before the United States International Trade Commission (USITC). If your copyright or trademark is registered, it can also be recorded with the CBP. The CBP can use enforcement procedures to prevent the entry of goods that infringe your IP rights into the USA. This is a simple and cost- effective measure to protect and enforce your IP rights. If you find unauthorized use of copyright material online, you can use the notice and takedown procedure to remove this material. This only works for websites owned in the USA and involves contacting the internet service provider with a demand to remove or disable access to the unauthorized content. With the help of a lawyer, you can also use a cease and desist letter. This warns an offender of your rights and asks them to stop any activity that may cause infringement. There are also several alternative dispute resolution (ADR) methods that can be used. These can involve mediation or arbitration and are often cheaper and faster than litigation. You may also find business associations and other industry-specific associations that can represent you in any dispute you may have involving unauthorized use of your IP.

Protecting your IP: You can do various things to make it harder for infringers to copy your product. For example, you could: Consider the design of your product and how easy it would be for somebody to reproduce it without seeing your original designs. Have effective IP-related clauses in employment contracts for when you hire staff. You should also make sure you educate your employees on IP rights and protection. Have sound physical protection and destruction methods for documents, drawings, tooling, samples, machinery etc. Make sure there are no 'leakages' of packaging that might be used by counterfeiters to pass off fake product. Check production over-runs to make sure that the genuine product is not being sold under a different name. Avoiding problems: The most important way to avoid problems when defending IP rights in the USA is to be prepared. To make sure that you can anticipate any potential issues, you should

- take advice from US IP rights experts by consulting publications and websites on US IP rights and protection in general
- carry out risk assessment and due diligence checks on any organizations and individuals you deal with y take professional advice from other experts—e.g., lawyers, local diplomatic posts, business and industry specific associations and UK trade organizations
- Talk to other businesses already doing similar trading in the USA.
- Consult agents, distributors, and suppliers on how best to safeguard your rights.
- Check with the trademark or patent attorneys to see whether there have been previous registrations of your own IP in the USA.
- Stick to familiar business methods; don't be tempted to do things differently because you're trading in different countries.

CHAPTER 12

REFERENCES! CURRENT ECONOMY OF USA (MAY, 2021 TO ONWARD)

Consumers shook off the pandemic blues as 2021 began, putting stimulus checks to figure , buying cars and other goods, and helping set the stage for what might be the fastest economic process in decades.

The initial reading on the country's first-quarter economic performance, delivered Thursday by the Department of Commerce, showed that much remained far away from normal. Even with an enormous jump in income, there was only a modest increase in spending on services like travel, dining, and even health care.

But economists say that's already changing as more vaccinations are delivered, and corona virus-related business restrictions are eased. With better weather, savings accumulated during an extended year of lockdowns, and an itch to form up for forced inactivity, Americans will have many reasons to travel out and spend.

"Consumers are now back within the driver's seat when it involves economic activity, and that's the way we love it ," said Gregory Daco, chief

U.S. economist at Oxford Economics. "A consumer that's feeling confident about the outlook will generally spend more freely."

Overall, the broadest measure of the economy's gross domestic product grew by 1.6 percent within the first three months of 2021, compared with 1.1 percent within the final quarter of last year. On an annualized basis, the first-quarter rate of growth was 6.4 percent.

The total economic output should return to pre-pandemic levels by summer. In fact, Mr. Daco believes it's already done so. His firm estimates that the economy will expand by 3.1 percent within the second quarter or about 13 percent annually. For the year, it expects growth of seven .5 percent, the simplest performance since 1951.

"This could also be the tip of the iceberg," Mr. Daco said. "I think we'll see much stronger momentum into summer as health conditions still improve, policy support remains in situ , and employment strengthens."

Helped by several rounds of state relief payments, households were sitting on a collective $4.1 trillion in savings within the half-moon , up from $1.2 trillion before the pandemic began.

That should find its way into the economy as services that were mostly off-limits come to life and customers flock to reopened establishments. Mr. Daco expects consumer spending to grow by quite 9 percent this year, a record.

The expansion last quarter was spurred by two batches of government payments to most Americans $600 a person from a relief package enacted just before the end of 2020 and $1,400 more from legislation approved in March. That quickly translated into purchases of cars, furniture, and household appliances, as well as clothes and food.

There was a similar jump in income last year after the first round of relief checks, which also caused a bounce in spending on goods.

"To some extent, when people have money, they're going to spend it," said Ben Herzon, executive director of IHS Market, a forecasting firm. "If they're not spending on services because they're not going to movies or amusement parks, they're going to derive utility from goods."

He said he expected spending on goods to ease in the second quarter as services spending begins to rebound more strongly.

Consumer spending rose 2.6 percent in the first three months of the year, with a 5.4 percent increase in purchases of goods accounting for most of the growth. Spending on services, which has slumped throughout the pandemic, rose by 1.1 percent.

"This demonstrates the value of government intervention when the economy is on its knees from Covid," said Ian Shepherdson, chief economist at Pantheon Macroeconomics. "But in the coming quarters, the economy will be much less dependent on stimulus as individuals use the savings they've accumulated during the pandemic."

The economy's underlying strength has been evident in the robust corporate earnings that many companies have reported in recent days. After the stock market closed Thursday, Amazon announced that its profit more than tripled last quarter to over $8 billion, while sales jumped 44 percent to $108.5 billion.

One striking aspect of the quarter's economic activity was spending on motor vehicles and parts, which increased by almost 13 percent from the previous three months. Strong consumer demand and tight inventories drove prices higher.

Low-interest rates, readily available credit, rising home values, stock prices, and strong trade-in values for used models also ease consumers' paths. At AutoNation, the country's largest dealership chain, many vehicles are being sold near or at sticker price even before they arrive from the factory. "These vehicles are coming in and going right out," said Mike Jackson, the chief executive.

Even if the economic output is back to where it was before last year, as Mr. Daco estimates, it is short of where it would be without the pandemic. What's more, economists say it is likely to take until sometime next year for employment to regain the ground it lost due to the pandemic.

The labor market underscores the uneven distribution of economic pain. White-collar employees have been able to make a smooth transition to working from home and relying on services like Netflix and DoorDash for their needs, but blue-collar workers and less-educated Americans have been hit hard. And while household savings over all have swelled, many families have seen their finances wiped out.

The unemployment rate for high school graduates was 6.7 percent in March, while it stands at 3.7 percent for Americans who hold a college degree. Members of minority groups have also suffered heavily, with the jobless rate for Black Americans at 9.6 percent, compared with 5.4 percent for whites.

Still, hiring does seem to be catching up. Last month, employers added 916,000 jobs and the unemployment rate fell to 6 percent, while initial claims f o r unemployment benefits have dropped sharply in recent weeks. On Thursday, the Labor Department reported that initial claims for state unemployment benefits had fallen to the lowest level of the pandemic for the third consecutive week.

Tom Gimbel, chief executive of LaSalle Network, a recruiting and staffing firm in Chicago, said: "It's the best job market I've seen in 25 years. We have 50 percent more openings now than we did pre-Covid."

Hiring is stronger for junior to midlevel positions, he said, with strong demand for professionals in accounting, financing, marketing and sales, among other areas. "Companies are building up their back-office support and supply chains," he said. "I think we're good for at least 18 months to two years."

Ample savings and rising consumer optimism are giving businesses the confidence to bet on the future as well. Business investment rose 2.4 percent in the first quarter and surpassed its prepandemic level. Residential construction spending rose 2.6 percent.

Economic growth would have been even stronger had it not been for a fall in inventories, said Michael Gapen, chief U.S. economist at Barclays. Supply chain constraints and shortages of parts like semiconductors are causing halts in production, he said, most notably in the automobile sector.

He added that that should ease in the months ahead, especially as businesses take their cue from more bullish consumers.

"We're at the opening stages of what could be a solid six to nine months for the U.S. economy as it emerges from the pandemic," he said. "The best is still yet to come."

This page was unintentionally left blank.

CONCLUSION:

The advantages of a market economy include increased efficiency, productivity, and innovation. In a truly free market, all resources are owned by individuals, and the decisions about how to allocate such resources are made by those individuals rather than governing bodies.

According to the foregoing analysis, globalization is not merely an intensification of global interconnectedness brought about by market forces and technological change. Rather, it is a worldview shaped by capital and hegemonic power that aspires to establish a global system in line with the interests of capital.

The Internet will produce significant cost savings in many sectors of the economy, resulting in faster productivity growth. It will also produce lower prices for consumers, resulting in faster growth in living standards.

Globalization has changed the role of the state politically because of strengthened interstate relationships and dependence on one another. Thus, the state's role has changed from being an authoritative figure to a dependent figure relying on others making decisions or making decisions based on other's beliefs.

- It encourages private initiative.
- There is freedom of choice.
- It ensures that income is distributed equitably.
- It ensures economic development.
- It ensures job security and employment.
- Monopoly is prevented because of the joint participation in economic activities by both the private and public sectors.

This page was unintentionally left blank.

REFERENCES!

A) INTERNET:

(https://http://www.economicsdiscussion.net/government/taxation/canonsof-taxation-meaning-types-and-characteristics/17428

https://countryeconomy.com/gdp/usa

https://www.intelligenteconomist.com/economic-growth/ https://www.un.org/en/development/desa/policy/wess/wess_archive/searchable_ar%20chive/1948_WESS_Full.pdf

https://www.bls.gov/cpi/

https://www.international.gc.ca/gac-amc/campaigncampagne/g20/index. aspx?lang=eng

https://www.thebalance.com/how-does-the-u-s-economy-work-4056835

https://www.nap.edu/read/1101/chapter/14

https://www.economicshelp.org/blog/2634/economics/private-sector-vspublicsector/

https://gallagherhrcc.com/buildingbetter/ppc?matchtype=p&network=g&device=m&adposition=1t1&keyword=public%20sector&gclid=CjwKCAiA0svwBRBhEiwAHqKjFhcVsjBL-LsCKtwrMup M5OsluSFOKbur2hIkdE6uZ5SxoAa VL3I9RoCAZ0QAvD_BwE

https://www.tutor2u.net/economics/reference/private-sector-and-economicdevelopment

https://www.epi.org/publication/bp338-public-investments/
https://www.intelligenteconomist.com/factors-of-production
https://www.bloomberg.com › quicktake › full-employment)
https://tradingeconomics.com/united-states/
    unemployment-rate
https://tradepartnership.com/wp-content/uploads/2019/02/
    All-Tariffs-
StudyFINAL.pdf https://www.thebalance.com/
what-is-the-gross-nationalproduct- 3305847

B) BOOKS:

US China Economic Relationship
Economic Development in US
Financial Stability
The Wealth of Nations'
Financial Stability Report
Influence on US Economy
G20
CPI Index

C) LIST OF SYNONYMS AND ABBREVIATIONS!!!

ADR – American Depositary Receipt
AI – Artificial Intelligence
AM – Account manager
AOP – Adjusted Operating Profit
AOP – Annual Operating Plan
AP – Accounts payable
ARPU – Average revenue per user
ASP – Average selling price
AAA – Accra Agenda for Action
ABC – Agência Brasileira de Cooperação /Brazilian Agency for
    Cooperation
AP – Average Product

ARF – African Renaissance and International Cooperation Fund

AFC – Average Fixed Cost

AVC – Average Variable Cost

BOP – Balance of Payment

AU – African Union BASIC – Brazil, South Africa, India and China

BOD – Busan Outcome Document BRIC(S) – Brazil, Russia, India, China, (South Africa)

CIVETS Colombia, Indonesia, Vietnam, Egypt, Turkey and South Africa

DAC – Development Assistance Committee

DIRCO – Department of International Relations and Cooperation

ED – Elasticity of Demand

ES – Elasticity of Supply

EPA – Economic Partnership Agreement ERF – Emergency Response Fund (UN)

EU – European Union

FDI – Foreign Direct Investment

G7/8 – Group of Seven/Eight: Canada, France, Germany, Italy, Japan, United Kingdom, United States, (G7), including Russia (G8).

G20 – Group of Twenty: Argentina, Australia, Brazil, Canada, China, France, Germany, India, Indonesia, Italy, Japan, Mexico, Russia, Saudi Arabia, South Africa, South Korea, Turkey, United Kingdom, United States and the European Union.

GDP – Gross Domestic Product Surviving in a Buoyant Economy

GNI – Gross National Income

HLF – High Level Forum on Aid Effectiveness

IAPD – Indian Agency for Partnership in Development

IC – Indifference Curve

IBSA – India, Brazil and South Africa

ICFD – International Conference on Financing for Development

IMF – International Monetary Fund

LRAC – Long Run Average Cost

LRMC – Long Run Marginal Cost

LIC – Low Income Country (World Bank definition)

MC – Marginal Cost

MP – Marginal Product

MR – Marginal Revenue

MRPL – Marginal Rate of productivity of labor

MRS – Marginal rate of Substitution

MRT – Marginal Rate of Transformation

MDG – Millennium Development Goal

MIC – Middle Income Country (World Bank definition)

MU – Marginal Utility

NEPAD – New Partnership for Africa's Development

ODA – Official Development Assistance

OECD – Organization for Economic Co-operation and Development

PD – Paris Declaration

PPF – Production Possibility Frontier

PPS – Production Possibility Set

PPC – Production Possibility Curve

PPP – Purchasing Power Parity

RTS – Returns to Scale

SAC – Short Run Average Cost

SMC – Short Run Marginal Cost

SAARC – South Asian Association for Regional Cooperation

SADC – Southern African Development Community

SADPA – South African Development Partnership Agency

SSA – Sub Saharan Africa

SSC – South-South-Cooperation

TC – Total Cost

TVC – Total Variable Cost

TFC – Total Fixed Cost

TU – Total Utility

UN – United Nations
UNDP – United Nations Development Programme
USD – US-Dollar
USMCA – United States-Mexico-Canada Agreement
WP-EFF – Working Party on Aid Effectiveness
WTO – World Trade Organization

This page was unintentionally left blank.

AUTHOR INFORMATION

DR. JOSEPH GLASGOW:

- With an intense focus on business, creativity and innovation, Dr. Joseph Glasgow has had over fifteen years of management experience in both the public and private sector.
- He has explored his thoughts and innovations in both domestic and global travels. Today, Dr. Glasgow is self-employed on his own at Glasgow & Associates - Project Management Consultant.
- Dr. Glasgow has successfully contributed to the growth of several start-up ventures into full-fledged businesses by way of exceeding shareholders expectation, in addition to landing a high credit rating with…
- Dr. Glasgow guided one of New York municipality economic development agency, promoted trade agreements with Foreign Direct Investors (FDI); ensure municipality AAA moody credit rating. ➢ Further, Dr. Glasgow spent thirteen years in academia, facilitated undergraduate and graduate business courses—a profession he enjoyed immensely

EDUCATION:

- Earned a PhD in Business administration/International Business from the North central University,
- Masters in Science Administration (MSA) from the Central Michigan University, Masters in Project Management (MPM) from the Western Carolina University,
- Bachelor of Science (BSc) in Economic & Management.
- Diploma: Computer Technology – Control Data Institute
- Diploma: Supply Chain Management – Allison Institute
➤
- Apart from the aforementioned professional roles, Dr. Glasgow is heavily involved in his community—Church activities, YMCA, Meditation, and the Kennedy Carter Center, also giving speeches on topics such as economic empowerment, globalization and trade.
- Additionally, Dr. Glasgow presently facilitates online (undergraduate/graduate) business courses at institutions of high learning both domestic and global.
- Dr. Glasgow is a board member of the following organizations:
- American Arbitration Association: Triad international Business Council (North Carolina): United Nations Association (Charlotte North Carolina): Previously-New York State-Lemon Law (Arbitrator/Mediator) Center for Dispute Settlement: North Carolina State Notary Association:

www.ingramcontent.com/pod-product-compliance
Lightning Source LLC
Chambersburg PA
CBHW040856210326
41597CB00029B/4871